38 Apartment Real Estate

Reginald C. Fenton

TRAFFORD

© Copyright 2002 Reginald C. Fenton. All rights reserved.

No part of this publication may be reproduced, stored in a retrieval system, or transmitted, in any form or by any means, electronic, mechanical, photocopying, recording, or otherwise, without the written prior permission of the author.

Printed in Victoria, Canada

National Library of Canada Cataloguing in Publication Data

Fenton, Reginald C., 1932-
 38 years in apartment real estate / Reginald C. Fenton.
ISBN 1-55395-305-3
 I. Title. II. Title: Thirty-eight years in apartment real estate.
HD1394.F45 2002   333.33'85'068   C2002-905329-3

This book was published *on-demand* in cooperation with Trafford Publishing.
On-demand publishing is a unique process and service of making a book available for retail sale to the public taking advantage of on-demand manufacturing and Internet marketing.
On-demand publishing includes promotions, retail sales, manufacturing, order fulfilment, accounting and collecting royalties on behalf of the author.

Suite 6E, 2333 Government St., Victoria, B.C. V8T 4P4, CANADA
Phone   250-383-6864   Toll-free   1-888-232-4444 (Canada & US)
Fax   250-383-6804   E-mail   sales@trafford.com
Web site   www.trafford.com   TRAFFORD PUBLISHING IS A DIVISION OF TRAFFORD HOLDINGS LTD.
Trafford Catalogue #02-1020   www.trafford.com/robots/02-1020.html

10   9   8   7   6   5   4   3   2   1

Thirty-Eight Years in Apartment Real Estate

Table of Contents

Preface 3
Dedication 5
Acknowledgements 7
Prelude 9
Introduction : How I Started with Almost Nothing 11

Chapters

1. My First Property   Woodland Park 15
2. My Second Property   Queen Anne 21
3. My Third Property   Francis Avenue 24
4. My Fourth Property   Northfield Block 29
5. My Fifth Property   Next Door Fremont 40
6. My Sixth Property   Daytona Apartments 44
7. My Seventh Property   Dayton Apartments 52
8. Money Makers 60
    What 60
    Where 63
    Why 63
9. How I Found Money Makers 65
    How I Bought Them 65
10. The Park Apartments 67
    How I Bought It 67
    Fire and Housing Code Work 69
11. I Quit My Job at 43, now its full time 76

12. How I bought the Woodlawn Crest 78
13. How Big Do I Want to Be? 82
14. Camano Island Waterfront Summer Home 84
15. How I Bought the Lilli Anne Apartments 88
16. How I Bought the Juliana Apartments 90
    1031 Exchange 91
17. Maintenance, Repairs and Improvements 94
    Roofs 94
    Plumbing 96
    Electrical 102
    Water Heaters 103
    Refrigerators and Stoves 104
    Washers and Dryers 107
    Tuckpointing 107
    Flooring 108
    Painting and Caulking 109
    Vinyl Thermopane Windows 110
    Wallpaper Repair, Texturing .110
18. Policy: Smoking, Waterbeds, Pets 114
19. Tenant Screening 116
20. Rents: Grace Period, Pay or Move, Raises, Deposits . .119
21. Inspection Criteria, What I Look for 126
22. Money makers- even in Monticito, California 128
23. Drug Activity- Threat of Abatement 130
24. Then vs Now 135
25. Summary 137

Preface

I quit my job at 43 to write my own paychecks and maintain and manage my rental properties.

This book describes how I started with almost nothing and reached my goal in 11 years, which was to be financially independent. I did this by investing in older style apartment buildings and stores in Seattle, Washington.

You will see many pictures of buildings I bought, how I operated, maintained, improved, and sold some. Many anecdotes and examples are presented. Also pictures of my rewards along the way. You will learn what I think "money makers" are: why, where they are, and how I bought them.

Many tips, maintenance and repair techniques are described. You will learn the same opportunities are here today in every city in the United States if you buy right.

It's been my life for 38 years and it's been fun and rewarding.

Dedication

This book is dedicated to those people who are dissatisfied with their jobs, living from paycheck to pay check. To those that want to be their own boss, become financially independent, and control their investments themselves. To those that overcome the negative thinking and remarks from others. To those that are willing to put there hard earned money up to buy an apartment building after careful though analysis and inspection. Hopefully this book will help guide you along the way.

Acknowledgements

I thanked my wife, Charlene, a year or so before she passed away in 1984, for helping me fulfill my dream. After our first building she had confidence in me and would sign any deal I asked. Her interest was medicine and patient care. She went back to school and got her degree in nursing and took the State of Washington exam for Registered nurses and passed in the top 10% that year 1968. The apartment business was not her style but she was always supportive and helped me with many decisions involving decorating, paint colors, tenant selection, deposit refunds, rent raises, etc. It was just nice to talk with her at the end of the day over a cup of coffee. She was very bright and had a good sense of what was the right thing to do.

I thank my four children who all went with me at times to help out at the apartments. They each started helping me when they were 5 or 6 years old but at 14 or 15 they had other interests. I thank my 2 sons John and Jim, my 2 daughters Lori and Karon. John is in his last year of Criminal Justice at Seattle U. Jim sells Real Estate and has rentals in Everett, WA. Lori is a mental health counselor at the Monroe Prison. Karen is a consultant to several insurance companies and is President of the University Rotary Club this year, 2002.

I thank Al Chapman of Pioneer Realty who helped get me started and was a source of good advice for many years.

I thank my many tenants who helped me pay-off the buildings.

I thank my girl friend Jan Nielsen who encouraged me to write this book

I thank Trafford in Victoria B.C., for the printing, promotion and advertising on the Internet.

Prelude

In 1964 I got one idea from a book that changed my life for the next 38 years. This book is my way of giving something back to a life I've enjoyed: being my own boss, owning my own money, and the freedom to do things my way.

I've been a "hands on" apartment operator as opposed to a passive part time investor. I did the work myself or was always there when contracting work. What I've learned might be lost or forgotten if I did not write it down. I want to pass on to my family and anyone else interested in how I did it. I don't mean to give advise, others are more qualified, this is just how I did it.

Probably most people write books to make money. I've already made the money, profits if any will go to charity.

Introduction

How I Started With Almost Nothing

In 1963 I worked at Boeing, had a wife and three children, a house at the south end overlooking Lake Washington, 10417 76th Ave So. I felt very insecure, afraid of losing my job at Boeing. I was hired from California in January of 1960 and six months later when we got our drawings in the shop for the Minuteman Ground Support Equipment Boeing started laying people off. I wanted a part time job or investment to supplement my income and be able to save for my families future but all I was doing was living paycheck to pay check.

In October of 1963 Boeing sent me to Melbourne, Florida on a subcontract for the Minuteman Program. We rented our house and Boeing moved us to Florida for a one-year assignment. My wife was irritable all the time we were in Florida. She hated the hot, humid weather and the bugs. One morning the lady next door opened her front door to get the milk and paper and found a small rattlesnake coiled up on the porch. She just happened to have a piece of plywood inside next to the front door so she through the plywood on top of the snake and then jumped up and down on the plywood until the snake was crushed. She had a small child crawling on the floor nearby. Now my wife was afraid of snakes and fearful our 3 children would run into one. Consequently, to get away from my wife's irritability I spent many hours at the beach with the kids. Then we started going to the library, the kids and I. At the library I found a book that changed my life. The book was by Nickerson titled "How I turned $1000. Into a million in Real Estate." When I read this book I thought, "WOW I CAN DO THIS". Real Estate seemed to fit me like a hand in a glove. It seemed the perfect road toward financial independence someday.

Thirty-Eight Years in Apartment Real Estate

The author and his first son James. Just back from Florida 1964

Stuart, Florida 1963 - fishing was great!

Now how was I going to get started with very little money? I didn't know anyone I could borrow a down payment from. As it turned out Boeing gave me a one-month's salary going to Florida as the Engineering Representative on a four-man team, and one month's salary bonus upon my return. When the job ended we took a few days vacation and drove up the East Coast to show the kids some of the historical sites they would soon learn about in history. In North Carolina a problem developed with the car that took one-half month's salary to repair it and a week to fix. Florida water will even rust the fillings out of your teeth and a tiny hole had rusted through the timing chain cover on our 1959 Buick causing water to run down into the oil pan which burned out the bearings. This was found after twice tearing down the engine and replacing the bearings, heads and all gaskets and oil. We finally arrived home, got settled in our house and I started reading the Seattle Times every Sunday looking for a small apartment building for sale. With the salary bonuses and by selling an inexpensive second car I had $2,500 saved. My wife was moaning and groaning how we would probably lose it all.

I contacted one particular Realtor in the University District whom I learned owned a few properties himself and he started showing me some older 4 and 5 unit places. Most of the properties were old run down converted houses that had been milked and rented to student groups for years, real junkers. I was looking for a building that would show a least a 15% return on my down payment after all expenses and the mortgage payment. See analysis sheet below. I never told Realtors this because I thought they would lose interest in me as a buyer. However the analysis data gave me a quick framework to evaluate income property.

I was very goal directed. I thought about being a landlord all the time. I even had dreams of collecting rents, working around my buildings and making improvements and repairs. I was always handy and could fix things if I had the required tools. The apartment business seemed perfect for me and I was ready to get started.

```
                        ANALYSIS DATA
       BLDG_____
       ADDRESS_____
       Yearly Gross Income------------      Projected----------
       Yearly fixed Expenses----------                ----------
              Elec.---------------------
              Water, Sewer, Garb.-------            ----------
              Heat----------------------            ----------
              Insurance-----------------            ----------
              Taxes---------------------            ----------
              Other---------------------            ----------
       Estimated Expenses:
              Vacancy 2% of gross
              income--------------------            ----------
              Repairs 4% of gross--------           ----------
              & Maintenance
       Gross yearly expense-----------               ----------
       Net Income---------------------               ----------
       Financing, mortgage etc--------               ----------
       Net yearly cash----------------               ----------
       Return %-----------------------               ----------

       Notes:
```

Analysis sheet

Chapter 1

My First Property - Woodland Park

After about 3 months of looking and trying to hang on to my down payment the Realtor called. He had a 5 unit at 4136 Woodland Park Ave N. Actually it turn out to be a duplex and a triplex on one lot. The triplex was a 1908 house that had been converted to a 2-bedroom apartment on the first floor, and a 1- bedroom and studio on the second floor. The garage had been converted into two 1-bedroom units with a laundry room on the south side. The conversions took place in 1932 and the apartments were now furnished including heat and all utilities included in the rents. Both were frame buildings with Brick-Tex siding, an insulated material used in the 1930's. Brick-Tex looks like granule coated composition shingles but with a brick like embossed pattern. The price we settled at was $25000. , $2500. Down, and a Real Estate Contract for 20 years at $165 mo. 7% interest. The apartments were all rented and they were easily re-rented all the time I owned the property, 17 years. The first year, after raising the rents approximately 10% and making some inexpensive improvements like paint and used carpet, I had almost my entire down payment back after making all expenses and the contract payment.

Now I had possession I had to learn how to operate and manage the property. One of the first problems was a 50-gal water heater leased from Washington Natural Gas had rusted out and was leaking. The water heater was installed in the basement of the converted house and I had a ceiling height space problem. The new leased water heaters were too tall to fit. The Gas Co. recommended installing two 30-gal heaters piped so they worked together. The total leased price was about the same as before so it was a good solution.

Thirty-Eight Years in Apartment Real Estate

I soon had to re-rent some of the apartments and I had problems collecting rents. One time I went into an apartment because the rent was one week late and I wanted to see if the tenant was still living there. The first thing I saw was a .45 automatic in a shoulder holster hanging from the bedpost headboard. I kept after him but I could never catch him there. The tenant was shortly thereafter arrested while robbing a market on Aurora Ave and I never did collect the rent.

When the two-bedroom on the first floor became available I decided to try to find some used carpeting because the hardwood floors were marred, scratched and stained. I found an ad in the paper for 40 yards of almost new carpeting for $50. I called on the ad and learned a couple in a large condo on Capitol Hill had just replaced the carpeting with a different color they preferred. The carpet for sale was a medium green I was told, so I went to see it. It was a high/low plush pattern and looked great. The owners just thought it was too good to discard. I was able to get the three rolls into my station wagon, drive to 4136 Woodland Park, back over the lawn and slide the carpet through the double doors of the 2-bedroom unit. I cut the carpet to fit the living room and dining room and tacked the perimeter down with small tacks. I also pieced the seam between the living room and the dining room with tacks. Since the carpet was about 5/8 inches thick I got by without using padding. The carpet looked great, the thickness hid the seam, and I rented the apartment for $25 more per month. There-after I installed a lot of good, used $1.00 a yard carpet in my rental units, in the above manner, sometimes using a kicker to stretch the carpet a little before tacking it down.

One time I had a couple in the two-bedroom unit that wouldn't respond to my notes requesting they pay their rent. I even sent them a letter stating I need my rents so I can pay my bills and the contract payment, still no response. They wouldn't even answer the door when I knocked. One morning I waited until they left for work and then I installed a hasp with a large padlock on both the front and rear doors. I then taped a sign on both doors that read "You are occupying this apartment illegally because you have not paid rent. If you break in I'll have you arrested for breaking and entering. Call me to

My First Property - Woodland Park

get inside and remove your things". That afternoon they called and I let them inside while they removed their personal property. Today I wouldn't even think of locking someone out because of all the new laws that favor the tenant, but it worked for me then. I didn't consider a court ordered eviction because I thought I couldn't afford the expense and delay.

Another time I had an ad in the paper for a 1-bedroom furnished apartment for rent and I got a call from a couple that had just got married and were staying in a hotel downtown for their honeymoon. They asked if I could pick them up and show them the apartment which I did. They liked the apartment so much they rented it on the spot, and wanted to move in that day after concluding arrangements. I took them back to their hotel. Their belongings consisted of suitcases and a large riding saddle and blanket. We loaded everything into my station wagon and moved them into the apartment. They lived there for over 11 years and raised 2 children there. When the second child came they rented the studio across the hall giving them the whole upper floor.

One time I got a call that the washer wasn't working. I furnished free washer and dryer service at that time. The washer was an old Maytag ringer type and the dryer was a gas Hamilton. The call came in shortly after dinner and as I was going out the door my wife said, "I'll go with you". I was under the washer; my wife was behind the laundry room door next to the dryer, when the tenant that called came in. First I smelled the perfume, then as she walked in I could see her in her nightgown, a pretty turquoise and she had red hair and blue eyes which made a pleasant sight. I never found a problem with the washer but my wife started going with me more often.

I later had to replace the washer because there was a switch you turned on to pump out the water and a tenant did their wash, rang it through the ringer then turned the switch on, and left it on which burned out the motor. I replaced the motor and then installed a coin box/ timer on the wall to shut off the washer automatically. The box took a dime for 1/2 hour.

Thirty-Eight Years in Apartment Real Estate

When I bought the property the triplex in front had a Coleman gas fired forced air furnace that worked well all the time I owned the building. The converted garage, upper and lower 1-bedroom duplex, was heated with separate Sigler space heaters. The gas was supplied to both buildings with one gas meter. This worked well for many years. In 1977 the cost of furnishing heat was increasing rapidly. I paid $1171 for heat the year before. I got the Gas Co. to install 5 separate gas meters which they did for free. Then, after 3 bids, I hired a contractor to install separate wall mounted heaters in the upper units of the triplex and the required gas piping. The piping to the Coleman furnace was already there so the heat ducts to the second floor were blocked off, and the furnace just heated the 2-bedroom apartment on the first floor. So now the tenants were paying their own heat bill with the separate meters with no change in their rent. The conversion cost $1117 so the installation paid for itself the first year.

One time I had a burst pipe at 2AM. I lived 1/2 hour away so I called the water dept and asked for emergency shut-off which cost $8.00 then and the water was promptly shut-off. I told the tenant that called reporting the leak that I would be there at 6AM. I found a pin head size hole had rusted through the supply line to the toilet resulting in water spraying around the bathroom. I installed a new line and almost made it to work on time. The water dept was a great help in getting the water shut-off quickly and thus preventing damage to the ceiling below.

Shown below is a picture of what the property looks like today, 2002. In 1981 I offered the property for sale. I placed a two line ad in the Seattle Times which read "Woodland Park, 5 unit, $90K, terms, owner 485-3007". I was overwhelmed with calls. I set up appointments whereby I would meet them at the Woodlawn Crest Apartments and drive them by the Woodland Park property. Also I gave them a handout shown below which lists income and expenses and proposed terms. I told them I didn't want to disturb the tenants and that I would only show the apartments upon receiving an Earnest Money and deposit. Several people submitted Earnest Moneys but after inspection said the apartments were too old. Other Earnest Moneys were lo-ball offers. I sold the property in April 1981

My First Property - Woodland Park

Author's first property - 4136 Woodland Park Ave N - Brick-Tex siding recently removed 2002

for $90000, $27500 down, $640 mo. 11%, 12 year cash-out. The owner paid it off early, 1991, and has kept the property up well. I believe the same buyer, Harold Ford owns it today 2002 and has done well. He has been stripping off the old Brick-Tex siding and painting the wood underneath. The wood has been covered since 1930 so it's in good condition. He is also replacing the old double hung windows and casings with new windows.

Years ago Hartney Oakes who I bought the Park Apartments from, and had been in the business since he was a youngster working for his mother, said to me "Fenton when you sell a building always leave something for someone else or you run the risk of taking it back. " Hartney was my mentor.

Thirty-Eight Years in Apartment Real Estate

```
FOR SALE...BY OWNER                          Reginald C. & Charlene
                                             E. Fenton
5 UNITS . . . 4136 & 4136½ Woodland Park Ave N   19934 80th NE
                                             Bothell, Wn 98011
    • Separate Heat                          485 3007
    • Partial Basement
    • Laundry Facilities
    • Gas Heat & cooking

Price: $90,000.00, $25,000. Down, balance $65,000. 1st T.D. 10%
       interest, re-establish interest rate at 5, 10, and 15 year
       intervals from date of closing, re-establish to market level.

FINANCIAL ANALYSIS:

Rent Schedule                        1 May 1981        Re-rent
                                                       Estimate
    4136        2 Bedroom               $200             $290
    4136½ Apt A Studio                   140              160
      "    "  B 1 bedroom                165              185
      "    "  C 1 bedroom                160              185
      "    "  D 1 bedroom                160              185
    Laundry                               20 est           20
                                        ─────            ─────
              Total Monthly              875             1025
              Income

ANNUAL INCOME & EXPENSES
                                     Current         Projected
ANNUAL INCOME                        $10500.00       $12300.00

ANNUAL FIXED EXPENSES:

    Real Estate Taxes                 674.73           900.00
    Personal Property Tax              13.02            13.02
    Insurance                         103.00           150.00
    Electric                          145.25           145.25
    Water                              81.25            90.00
    Sewer                             131.80           143.00
    Garbage                           289.98           300.00
    Gas for hot water                 500.00 est       600.00

              Total Expenses         1939.03          2341.27

              1st TD payments        6120.00          6120.00
Proposed terms, 20 years approx.
$510/mo 2 yrs, $600/mo 3 yrs, then
$650/mo thereafter

ANNUAL NET INCOME                    $8560.97         $9958.00

Annual net cash                      $2440.97         $3839.73




OWNER MUST BE PRESENT FOR INSPECTION - DO NOT DISTURB
TENANTS.
```

1981 sale terms

Chapter 2

My Second Property - Queen Anne

In 1965 I got a call from my Real Estate friend Al Chapman. He had a upper and lower duplex for sale at 2540 7th Ave W. on the top of Queen Anne 1&1/2 blocks north of the Coe Elementary school. While inspecting the units I saw a piano in the owners unit with a picture of a gentleman I worked with at the Bremerton Naval Shipyard in 1956, Mr. Sullins. His wife was selling the duplex as he had passed away shortly before. I was surprised at the coincidence as we were friends and belonged to the same Masonic Lodge.

I purchased the duplex for $10500 with a minimum down FHA loan (almost closing costs) for 30 years, 5&3/4 %. Upon closing the property and taking possession I found a storage shed was missing from the back yard, also both screen doors and a light fixture from the owners unit. It was a nice shed, about the size of a small I car garage. The agent called the seller and she said the shed was a portable building on skids so they skidded it onto a flatbed truck and hauled it away. She did however return the screen doors and light fixture.

I got a call one-day from the tenant in the lower unit. She said the electric meter outside her dining room window was very noisy with a grinding sound. I said I would call City Light. She called back later and said City Light people inspected the meter and said it was just a noisy meter. As they were returning to their vehicle the meter started smoking and caught fire. City Light quickly put out the fire and replaced the meter. Next time I was there I touch-up painted around the meter socket so if an Insurance Inspector or Fire Inspector came by it wouldn't be cause for alarm.

One time when I had a vacancy in the upper unit I had an applicant that upon reviewing his application told me he was gay. He also said "if I didn't rent to him he would own the building". I laughed at that and continued interviewing him with his application in my hand. I had just installed some nice used carpeting so I wanted to be careful whom I rented to. He had been at his last two apartments for about a year each. He had a good job as a waiter in a good restaurant downtown for 2 years. He had no pets and was ready to pay his rent and deposit in advance. I took a deposit from him subject to checking his references, which checked out. Also, he didn't have a car and the bus to his work stopped in front of the duplex so overall the apartment suited him well so I rented to him.

He was there over a year but left suddenly before his rent was up, and left the apartment needing cleaning. He left a note as to where he was, an address in Bishop California where he said a gay community living situation was his reason for leaving. I charged him for the cleaning and returned most of his deposit. I never had a problem with gays, neither men nor women- both have been among my better tenants.

About 5 years after I purchased the duplex I noticed the roof on the south side was curling and had wear spots where the granules had worn off. The south side was the prevailing weather side so the north side was in good condition. It was a steep roof, A-frame style with almost another story to achieve the slope. The roof while shot on the south side wasn't leaking into the upper apartment because of the steep slope. It was however, leaking between the plies and running down and dripping out the eves behind the gutter. Again, this deterioration was only on the south side. I found a Dutch Lap style roofing material was installed over the original wood shingles so I decided to install another roof on top of what was there. I got 3 bids and had a roofer install new Dutch Lap Shingles on the south side only, which saved ? the cost of a new roof. The north side still looked good approximately 21 years later when the building was remodeled.

All the time I owned the duplex, one apartment paid the mortgage, property taxes and all expenses. The other apartment was pure prof-

My Second Property - Queen Anne

it. In 1985 I sold the property to a tenant that had lived there a long time. The price was $68000, $6000 down, $740 a month, 11% interest. In 1991 the buyer got a new loan to completely remodel the building so he cashed out the principal balance, $39561.

Chapter 3

My Third Property - Francis Ave.

Again I got a call from my Real Estate friend Al Chapman. He had 2 duplexes on 1 lot for sale at 4320-24 Francis Ave N. The owner was a used car salesman trying to get into the apartment business. Before that a group of doctors owned it but the property was really run down. Leaky roofs in both buildings and also the garage roof on the north side of the front building leaked profusely. The yard at one time probably looked real nice with what looked like a small mountain, concrete and rock, with a waterfall at the top, running down the front into a pond. The yard was very overgrown; grass a foot high, many weeds, too many large trees with their branches chafing the power lines and rubbing against the sides of the buildings. All the bushes shrubs and hedges needed trimming and cutting back. Also, upon inspecting the foundation I found infestation; powder post beatles, termites, and carpenter ants.

I decided to not purchase the property because of the infestation. The broker however offered to give up part of his commission toward the infestation problem and to help the sale. I than went ahead and purchased the property for $26000, $4610 down, $150, 7% on contract. On closing I received $840 back because of the infestation.

First I fixed the leaky roofs. I had little experience then fixing roof leaks and I didn't have mountain climbing safety equipment as I later bought and used on other buildings, so I hired a roofer. The front building had a steep roof and only the rear dormer, porch area was leaking, and the sides were in good condition, so I had the roofer put new 3-tab composition shingles over the old. The rear building had

My 3rd Property - Francis Ave.

a hot tar built up roof with little slope. The leaks were around the drain scuppers where there was standing water. The roofer hot mopped felt around the scupper areas which fixed the leaks.

Shortly thereafter I hired the same roofer that did the 3-tab shingle work to install a new roof on my house. He and a helper did a good job at an excellent price, just "banged it out" in about 16 hours. I learned he committed suicide about a year later. He was such a big strong guy with a nice easy- going personality that I found it hard to believe. I also learned it had to do with depression. I liked him and really felt sad. And even today I feel sad he probably didn't have the understanding and help that is available today.

The lower unit was vacant in the front building. Apartments were difficult to rent and both buildings were semi furnished. The lower front apartment had almost no furniture so I wanted to rent it "as is". Both duplexes had separate meters for each unit so they paid there own for heat, cooking and hot water. I put a large sign in the front window of the lower unit, which read $59, and my phone number. Right away I had several people apply. I rented the apartment to 2 older sisters that had always lived together, never married. The only problem I had with the sisters was their dishrag dept going down the kitchen sink drain line and stopping up the sink. Many times I got the call and drove there (1/2 hour away to clear their sink line with my snake and each time I would pull back their dishrag.

The problem was the sink strainer basket didn't have a crosspiece so I replaced the basket. I now replace the basket in all sinks where the crosspiece is missing. Many times it corrodes away, breaks off or the plumber takes it out because he likes the 1/2 inch diameter ball at the end of his snake, which won't pass through the crosspiece.

After fixing the roofs and renting the vacant apartment I started looking into the infestation problem. I got bids from 3 bug contractors who all recommended using Cloridane injected into the foundation posts and floor joist where applicable, and spraying a 3 foot band of Cloridane around the building perimeter. As it turned out I found the Powder Post Beatle problem was very localized. The beatles were

Thirty-Eight Years in Apartment Real Estate

in only in a few of the posts. I tore out the 8"X 8" posts and replaced with new lumber. I found Carpenter Ants and Termites on the north foundation wall where there was 2 plugged downspout drains causing wet wood. I cleared the drains, replaced the infested wood, and sprayed Chlordane around the basement area, also a band around the outside perimeter. I never had any evidence of infestation after that.

Chlordane was banned at the time by the Environmental Protection Agency with the exception that present stocks could be used up. I found a half gallon in an old hardware / feed store in Woodinville that cost me $14.95. I still have most of it today and use it to spray around my beach house on Camano Island where Carpenter Ants are abundant.

Next, in my priority, I tackled the overgrown yard problem and almost lost my life. I started by removing several trees and trimming branches on other trees that were encroaching on the power lines, walkways, and rubbing against the buildings. I used an aluminum ladder to accomplish access to the limbs and I was about 8 feet up on the ladder when I stepped off the ladder to cut a large limb with my chain saw. The limb was entwined with the power lines to the rear duplex. Suddenly the limb fell and the 3 lines wrapped around my perspiring shoulder and neck. The power lines were bare copper wire in places due to the limbs chafing and removing the insulation. If I hadn't just stepped off the aluminum ladder I would have been electrocuted. As it was the bare lines touched the ladder and "bang", sparks flew and tripped a breaker on the power pole at the street. I was able to trim the rest of the limbs and branches more safely until City Light arrived to restore power to the neighborhood. City Light advised me they would have temporarily cut power to my building if I had called them- something I will always remember to do.

A tenant I eventually rented to was Garnet Seeley, a retired telephone operator at the Seattle Times for 31 years. She was a single lady, never married and she passed away about a year after she moved in. I received a call from an attorney advising me of her death and to say the rent would not be paid for the following month and

My 3rd Property - Francis Ave.

Francis Ave. 2002

asked if I would like to submit a bid on her personnel property inside the apartment as there were no heirs. This was a 1-bedroom that was then unfurnished. He asked if I had an inventory list, and I said no, except for the stove and refrigerator. I inspected the apartment, made an inventory list and made a minimum bid based on what I could sell the items for at a garage sale. The only things worth anything were a TV set and a fur coat. The bid was quickly accepted by the attorney but now the fur coat was missing from the apartment. I then called the attorney and asked about the missing fur coat. He said "Fenton, your making a big deal out of this, I know nothing about a fur coat." I then asked if he was going to return his key to the apartment, he said he would but never did. After disposing of her things I felt sad that her whole life's possessions were in that apartment including an old trunk full of letters, keepsakes, etc all of no value except a phallic vibrator, TV and a fur coat.

Next I thought I had a chance to buy another building nearby, the Northfield Block, but I needed to raise some more money for the

Thirty-Eight Years in Apartment Real Estate

Ad used to sell Francis Ave. in 1968

expected down payment. So I listed Francis Ave with Al Chapman of Pioneer Realty in 1968. The ad shown above was the asking price. It sold for close to that price and I got cashed out and paid the full commission. The buyer assumed the underlying contract on the property.

Chapter 4

My Fourth Building - The Northfield Block

In November of 1967 my Real Estate friend Al Chapman called. He found a brick building at 4250 - 56 Fremont Avenue N. There were 4 large stores, 1500 sq. ft., each on the first floor and 4 large apartments, 1500 sq. ft. each above the stores, with full basements below the first floor. The sale wasn't listed with anyone - it was an open listing being sold by an attorney because it was an estate situation and there were minor children involved. We submitted an Earnest Money for $45,000 (which the attorney indicated was what they wanted) payable $8,000 down on a Real Estate Contract, $305 per month at 7% interest. This was acceptable to the attorney and the seller and was accepted in April 1968 with the counter offer that I would buy on a net basis. This meant I would pay costs of Title Insurance, State Excise Tax (1%) and Real Estate Commission (6%). I agreed to this counteroffer. We each paid 1/2 of the escrow fee to Security Title. Pioneer Realty agreed to loan me the commission on an Installment note for $2,700 payable at $25 per month, 6% interest for 2 1/2 years, then $75 per month thereafter. We, my wife and I, signed a "Purchaser's assignment of Real Estate Contract and Deed" to secure the note to the lender. Six years later I received the note back marked "paid in Full" which I promptly recorded at the courthouse.

During escrow it was learned the house at the rear of the property was included in the sale - 712 N. Motor Place. I was able to negotiate a deed release for the house, lots 11 and 12 when the balance on the contract was less than $27,000. Gladys Northfield was the widow of the property owner together with her children so I bought the property from the original family that built the main building and house in 1909.

Thirty-Eight Years in Apartment Real Estate

The property had been for sale for over a year and many investors had turned it down because the main building had been condemned the year before because the west elevation was out of plumb. The ties that hold the brick façade to the wood framing had rusted out. The whole wall on 1/2 of the West Side was leaning to the west. Mrs. Northfield had hired a contractor to install 4 X 4 X 12 beams vertically about 10 feet apart with horizontal ties to clamp the bricks to the frame wall so she could sell the property. (This was a good solution until I sold it whereby the new owner installed less conspicuous horizontal ties and metal rosettes instead of beams.

When I took possession (April 1968) only 4 of the 8 units were rented in the brick building and the house was rented to a family. Sutton's Heath Center occupied 2 stores in the middle as shown in the photo. My first priority was to get the vacant units rented.

In 1968 stores were very hard to rent. There was far greater demand for reasonable rent apartments. Right away I was able to rent the 2 vacant upper apartments; one to 4 young people who were artist types who wanted the large, spacious 3 bedroom units with a large sunporch, and another apartment to a family of 4. Both corner stores had living quarters in the rear of the stores; 4250 at the south end of the building formerly "The Hungry Steer" restaurant (see photo) and the north store (4256). I tried for 2 months to rent the south storefront separate from the rear living quarters without success. While advertising the unit as a "storefront with living quarters" I received great response. Prospective tenants thought it neat to live in a storefront with living quarters in the rear. I immediately rented it to a single lady artist who lived and worked there for many years using the storefront for her artwork and paintings.

The north store (4256) also had living quarters in the rear but the plumbing was leaking from the overhead so bad it was unrentable. Also, the last tenants, a large family or several families removed the kitchen sink, bathroom sink, several light fixtures and the toilet when they were evicted for non-payment of rent. I replaced the toilet and bathroom sink. I had a contractor install new Formica on the kitchen countertop as it was shot. I then installed a new stainless steel dou-

My Fourth Building - The Northfield Block

Northfield block 1968

Rear view Northfield block 1968

House at 712 N Motor Place 1968

ble sink. I prefer installing stainless steel sinks as compared to porcelain because they last longer. Also, you cannot buy the quality cast iron porcelain sinks today like the ones made in the 1930s and 1940s. They use a different manufacturing process now, a baked enamel. Stainless steel sinks will dent but they don't chip and show stains or wear.

At the same time I was renovating and restoring the living quarters I hired a plumbing contractor to fix the plumbing leaks. The main problem was under the toilet of the upper apartment. The plumbing was lead piping. Also the lead 4" diameter elbow from the base of the toilet to the 4" diameter cast iron stack was lead. Lead tends to crack and crumble in places particularly on second floor apartments, probably because there is more minute movement there. The contractor installed a 4" diameter black ABS plastic elbow with respective couplings and elbows to connect the 1 1/2" and 1 1/4" waste lines from the upper kitchen and bathtub. The connections to the existing lead lines was made near the elbow by cutting the old lead lines and inserting them into the plastic elbows and piping with oakum material and a stainless steel adjustable clamp. This was a faulty connection and continued to leak because, of course, lead does not compress very well so you could not get a good seal at the joint. Efforts to get the contractor to fix the problem didn't work out so I learned how to do it myself. I bought some radiator hoses from an auto parts store that were just the right size to cut and couple the plastic piping to the lead piping with a stainless steel clamp on both ends at the joint. This was before they had Furn-Co rubber couplings for this purpose. Thereafter, I was always looking for used or new radiator hoses the size I needed.

While working on the couplings from the new plastic to the lead piping, suddenly water gushed from the bathtub waste line. Unknowingly, the tenant upstairs was home and had taken a bath earlier and had just decided to pull the plug in her tub so it flooded the lower unit. I spent the rest of the day mopping up the bath water. Now the apartment/storefront was ready to rent with new paint, new fixtures, and a new kitchen floor. My first qualified applicant was a Boeing Engineer, wife and kids who thought it neat to live in a storefront with 3 bedroom living quarters, so I rented to them.

My Fourth Building - The Northfield Block

House fixed up and another house moved in

Now all of the units, including the house and 2-car garage at the rear were rented and they continued to be easy to rent for the next 18 years. My return the first year was 18% of my down payment but that was minimized by the many repairs. The return got better and better every year I owned it.

The first winter 1969 I started having trouble with my roofs. The house was easy to repair when I found the source of the leaks which were around the chimney flashing and around the vent pipes. The brick building roof was originally a three-ply hot tar built up type covered with gravel the size of a pea. I found by sectioning the roof that the gravel had been removed and 2 plies of rag felt had been hot mopped with tar with a flood coat of hot tar on the top surface. The top surface was badly "aligatored" (looked like an alligator's back) in many places with many blisters and cracks though the first ply or more in places. With a full time job at Boeing and 4 kids at home I didn't know what to do but hire a roofer. Mrs. Northfield, the former owner, told me that American Roofing had done the last roof so I called them for a bid. I talked to Mike Shurehoff who said it needed glazing also to prevent further cracking so I hired him to patch the cracks with felt and hot tar and flood coat the entire top surface. This worked well for several years. Then I started getting leaks around the skylights. They were the original metal-framed skylights with wire glass installed in 1909. At first I used asphalt mastic to seal between the glass and the metal frame but I found the asphalt tended to dry out and crack at the joints due to thermal expansion. I found that coal tar mastic worked best. It stayed soft, pliable and maintained a more lasting seal. Years later when I learned how to repair and install roofs myself, I used aluminum fiber coating on top of the coal tar which helped the mastic last longer (see chapter on "Roofing").

In 1971 I was getting leaking through the brick mortar joints on the south wall. Water was leaking behind the bricks, running down inside the wall and dripping into the store ceiling and also into the basement plaster ceiling on the south side underneath the store. I hired a contractor Al Belmont to tuckpoint the south elevation from the top to about 1/2 way down. He rigged a stage from the roof and an old-time tuckpoint man named Mr. Poe made three drops with the stage and did the whole job himself. There were no leaks through the bricks after that. The job looks good today 2002.

Heat Conversions

The house at 712 N. Motor Place was heated by a diesel fired forced air heating system and a fireplace in the living room. One day the diesel burner stopped pumping fuel so I replaced the pump. It still wouldn't pump and fire because a pump will not pump water - there was water in the oil tank located underground. Water always goes to the lowest point in the tank. I could have installed another tank above ground but diesel systems require periodic maintenance and repair: cleaning the electrodes, replacing the filters both oil and air, adjusting the flame, etc. I contacted the Gas Company and they had a program whereby they would install a gas meter and the necessary piping to a rental gas fired burner which they maintained for free. All I had to pay was a small rental fee of $2.36 per month. Also at the same time I decided to upgrade the domestic hot water supply, which came from the main building. I signed a lease contract with Washington Natural Gas for a gas fired water heater. I capped the hot water line from the main building and the Gas Company hooked up the piping to the leased water heater. It only cost me $1.96 for the

My Fourth Building - The Northfield Block

water heater lease. The gas company did all the necessary piping and installation free.

In 1968 when I bought the Fremont package the main building furnished heat using hot water radiators in the apartments and stores. A new furnace had been installed years ago to upgrade from coal using Bunker C or PS 300 fuel which was crude oil direct from Saudi Arabia at $.09 per gallon. My heat bill for the first 4 years was $400 - $500 per year. The former furnace was a coal stoker, which required greater maintenance because someone had to be on hand to add coal periodically, the amount and frequency depending on the weather. This Ray burner conversion also upgraded the domestic water supply to the apartment/store units because the domestic supply was hooked up to a smaller coal stoker furnace, which was now abandoned. The Bunker C conversion employed a 200-gallon hot water tank piped into the main furnace heat exchanger to supply hot domestic water to the stores/apartment units.

In 1973 PS 300 black oil prices were rising. I was paying $1,200 per year instead of $500 in 1969. Also there was the daily maintenance of cleaning the burner nozzle which looked like the end of a fire hose. The nozzle sprayed out the black oil and a spark plug type igniter lit the flame. Carbon would build up on the nozzle and if not clean the oil would run into the firebox and down on the floor and catch fire. I had this happen only once. It produced a very black, smoky fire that brought the Fire Department to the building to extinguish the blaze.

Also, I would clean the furnace (boiler) firebox and furnace flues. This was accomplished by using a furnace wire brush on the end of a 6' rod and vacuuming the residual dust and scale with a shop-type vacuum. The result was better heat transfer to the hot water inside the furnace or sometimes called a boiler.

So again, PS 300 oil prices were rising and I wanted to reduce the maintenance. Washington Natural Gas also had a program for commercial buildings. They would install the gas meter, furnish a leased gas fired burner to replace the Ray oil burner and provide a leased gas fired water heater for the domestic water all at no charge. Also they provided free maintenance to service their equipment if necessary. All I had to do was sign the leases and pay $5.91 per month. Of course, I had to pay the natural gas cost but that was less that oil and I eliminated the maintenance. Now I had a good hot water heating system, both space heating and domestic hot water

In 1982 although I had a good heating system, it was costing me approximately $6,000 per year to furnish heat to the apartments/stores. Also, I had the problem of controlling the heat which required adjusting the thermostat depending on the weather.

I got several bids to convert the building to tenant paid electric heat. I selected a contractor who installed electric baseboard heat in the apartments and a combination of baseboard and electric heater/fan type units in the stores. Also a new service entrance with new meter sockets and new circuit breaker panels were added to each apartment and store. The cost was $15,594 complete. There was no reduction in rent. The tenants seemed to understand that heating prices had gone up considerably and now they were paying for what they used. This worked out to be a polite way of giving the tenant a rent raise as I was saving $6,000 (the first year). The conversion thus paid for itself in about 2 1/2 years.

In April of 1978, when the contract balance was less than $27,000 I was able to get a Partial Deed Release so I could sell the house 712 N. Motor Place. I sold it myself for $26,950, $5,390 down, balance $191 per month, 9 1/2% interest, cash out in 5 years. I agreed to continue furnishing cold water from the main building for 6 months to allow the buyer time to install a separate water meter and water line to the subject property. The buyer remodeled the house and sold it later. The photo shows the house on the right and a house that was moved onto the rear of the property. It was jacked up to build 3 units underneath which is shown in progress. Since it was commercial zoned, property setbacks from the property lines were not required which helped the project. The photos show the rear of the main building today 2002 with a similar view from 1968.
In 1986 I sold the Northfield Block to reduce my maintenance (see

My Fourth Building - The Northfield Block

Northfield block 2002

Rear view Northfield block 2002

Thirty-Eight Years in Apartment Real Estate

712 Motor Place house 2002 with tri-plex at rear

```
FOR SALE......BY OWNER                              Reginald C. Fenton
                                                    Jr
8 UNITS.......4 Stores, 4 Apts 4250-56 Fremont N    19934 80th NE
                                                    Bothell, Wn 98011
   • Rewired                                        483-5884 AFTER 4PM
   • Electric Heat
   • Full Basements

Price: $240,000. $70,000. Dn, bal $170,000. 1st TD 10% int. for 2 yrs
        at $1416 mo., then 11% $1700. mo thereafter, 15 yr C/O

FINANCIAL ANALYSIS:

Rent Schedule                          1 May 1985         Re-rent
                                                          estimate
    4250        Store w living qtrs      $275              $550
    4252        Store                     190               350
    4254        Store                     225               350
    4256        Store w living qtrs       290               500
    4250 Apt A  3 bedroom                 285               400
    4252  "  B  3 bedroom                 270               350
    4254  "  C  3 bedroom                 250               350
    4256  "  D  3 bedroom                 250               350
                                                            70 garage
                Total monthly            2035              3270
                income

ANNUAL INCOME & EXPENSES:              Current         Projected
ANNUAL INCOME                          $24,420.        $39,240.

ANNUAL FIXED EXPENSES

    Real Estate Taxes                  1637.33          1900.00
    Gas (hot water)                    1326.86          1500.00
    Insurance                           303.00           400.00
    Water & Sewer                       798.39           900.00
    Garbage                             539.30           600.00

                Total Expenses         4004.88          5300.00

                1st TD payments       16992.00         16992.00

Proposed terms, 25 years approx.
$1416 mo, 10%, 2 yrs
$1700 mo, 11%, thereafter, 15 yr C/O

ANNUAL NET INCOME                     $20,416.00       $33,940.00

Annual Net Cash                        $3224.00        $17,250.00


OWNER MUST BE PRESENT FOR INSPECTION.....DO NOT DISTURB TENANTS.........
```

Copy of handout I gave to prospective buyers

My Fourth Building - The Northfield Block

Chapter 13 "How Big Do I Want to Be?"). I sold it myself, placing an ad in the Seattle Times and handing out the data sheet shown on page 38 to prospective buyers. After several offers I would up selling the property to the contractor who installed the electric heat conversion, Burton Walls Electric. He, if course, had personal knowledge about the building and was my best buyer and he seemed to like to the property. The negotiated price was $230,000, $30,000 down, and $1,600 per month, 10% interest. The contractor has since done a good job of remodeling and upgrading the building. The photo on page 37 shows a front and rear view on Fremont Avenue of what it looks like today 2002, well maintained. I don't want to take the time to figure out the return each year, but it was 18.6% the first year after fixing a lot of deferred maintenance and repair. It only got better each year especially when you factor in the conversions. My oldest daughter Karon (see photo below) got her degree in Mathematics, is almost an actuary and likes math problems and accounting. I might ask her to determine the return on my down payment plus additional returns on the upgrades on a yearly basis. It was a moneymaker.

Oldest daughter Karon - Shilshole Bay - 1995

Chapter 5

My Fifth Property - 4258 – 62 Fremont Ave N.

In November 1968 I purchased the building next door to the Northfield Block. This building was a 4 unit; 2- stores on the street level and 2 2-bedroom apartments on the second floor above the stores. Also a 2 1/2 car garage at the rear of the property. All the units had their own gas meters and paid their own heat; Sigler space heaters in the two apartments and Reznor fan type ceiling mounted heaters in the two stores. Shown below is a picture of the building taken about 1930. The building looked better when I bought it in 1968 but it still looked shabby in appearance. I contacted the owner who owned a Fuel Oil Company in Lynnwood, Washington. There was one vacant 2-bedroom apartment and he seemed anxious to sell the property. I bought it for $23000, $2000, down, $200 month including taxes and insurance, 6 1/2 %. Shown below is my analysis of the property then. The owner had other business interests and it was just luck I contacted him at the right time. He'd had the building for sale through Real Estate for $26950. But it didn't sell. He was very easy to negotiate with and just an easy person to talk to. After closing he called me and said, "Fenton, if you ever have any trouble making payments to Century Savings & Loan (collection account) call me first"). I never did and paid the contract off in May of 1985.

I had good tenants all the time I owned the property. The north store was rented to a Detective Agency for many years and then to an Attorney/Oriental Rug dealer who is still there (2002). The other store was rented to the Pink & Pretty beauty shop for 22 years, then Der Har Fizor Barber Shop now in Ballard on Market St. I rented the

My Fifth Property – 4258 – 62 Fremont Ave N.

Fremont Ave 1930

2 1/2 car garage to a race car driver who was there many years. He improved the garage by adding insulation and 220 power to serve his welding equipment.

Upon possession, after getting the vacant 2-bedroom apartment rented I painted the front of the building a light beige and the tile a brick red. I re-painted using the same colors several times in the 27 years I owned the building.

One time I had a call about a leak around the base of the toilet in the Beauty Shop. I checked it out and found a tiny hairline crack in the wall mounted holding tank. I did this by putting red food coloring in the tank, which reveled itself on the bottom of the tank. I had a mediterranean blue toilet that I had purchased from the Salvation Army's "as is" department on 4th Ave (one of my favorite shopping places for parts at that time). The toilet costs $7.50 complete. The restroom in the Beauty Shop served both men and women so instead of pink or white I decided to install my blue toilet to replace the defective 2-piece wall mounted toilet.

41

```
                    -1968-        ANALYSIS DATA
        BLDG   2 STORES  2 APTS  2½ CAR GARAGE
        ADDRESS  4258-62  FREMONT AVE N.
                              $ 3960
        Yearly Gross Income----------         Projected----------
        Yearly fixed Expenses----------                 ----------
                                   151
                Elec.------------------
                                   138
                Water, Sewer, Garb.-------                ----------
                                   - 0 -
                Heat------------------
                                   (36)
                Insurance----------------                ----------
                                  (317)
                Taxes------------------
                                   - 0 -
                Other------------------
        Estimated Expenses:

                Vacancy 2% of gross       79
                income------------------
                                   158
                Repairs 4% of gross--------               ----------
                & Maintenance
                                   526
        Gross yearly expense----------               ----------
                                   3434
        Net Income------------------
                               2400 (INCL. TAXES & INS.)
        Financing, mortgage etc--------                ----------
                                   1034
        Net yearly cash-----------
                                  51.7%
        Return %------------------
                               OF DN. PMT.
```

Analysis Data

About 6 months later I got a call from the tenant requesting I replace the dark blue toilet with a white one. It seems a lady went to the restroom and soon started screaming. A small rat had entered the bowl of the toilet and was tickling her bottom. The rat could have entered via the sewer line, swimming through the trap, as some older toilets have 3" diameter throats. I replaced the toilet with a white one making it easier to spot a rat. (Still have the blue one but hesitate to use it).

In 1995 while inspecting the garage roof because I had a leak, I suddenly fell through the roof. On the way down my left arm caught a rafter, which kept me from falling to the concrete floor below. I had

My Fifth Property - 4258 – 62 Fremont Ave N.

several cracked ribs but no sharp pain so I used a wrapper type support for awhile. It hurt to even breathe at first but soon got better. I was unable to jog for about 3 weeks. I had remembered my wife (she was a RN) telling me that there is nothing Doctors do about cracked ribs except pain control and supports- letting them heal themselves. Since I carried my own insurance this is what I did.

I decided to replace the roof. With a helper we tore all the old roofing material off, installed several new rafters, installed 3/8" plywood sheets over the old deck, nailed a base sheet to the plywood, and installed torchdown material on top of the base sheet. This roof if properly maintained will last at least 40 years (see chapter on roof maintenance). I let a new torchdown roof season for 6 months to get rid of the talcum powder and residue then I aluminum fiber coat it.

In 1996 I sold the property through Real Estate for $295000, $50000 down, $1800 a month, 8%, 15 year cashout. I first placed a 2-line ad in the Seattle Times which read (" Fremont- 2-stores, 2-apts by owner" etc) but Real Estate brought me the best offer. Below is a picture taken shortly before I sold the building.

Fremont Ave 1996

Chapter 6

My Sixth Property - Daytona Apts.

After buying the 4258 Fremont building directly from the owner I started contacting other apartment house owners nearby. I just drove around the area my present properties were in: Woodland Park, Phinney Ridge, Wallingford and Fremont. I particularly spotted what I was beginning to think were "money maker" type buildings as described in Chapter 8. I made notes and jotted down addresses. Then I would call one of the Title Companies and obtain ownership information, when the property sold last, sale price, etc. I would then call the owner, tell them I liked their building and would they consider selling it now or in the future. The first call that paid off in early 1970 was the Daytona Apartments at 4504 Dayton Ave N. The owner had purchased the property in 1967 for $42500. It had been on the market recently for 6 months through Real Estate at $57500 or higher, but that was the price he was asking through Real Estate. Below is a copy of a data sheet he gave me as he was trying to sell it himself. The property had 4 large 1-bedroom apartments, a daylight basement studio, a sleeping room, and a double car garage on the north side, end to end. One access to the garage was from the street, the other from the alley. The building was heated with a diesel fired boiler with a side arm heat exchanger for the domestic or potable water and hot water radiators in each apartment.

I thought his price was too high but I kept in touch with him. Then one day I was driving by his building and it looked like there was 2 vacant apartments. As it turned I learned only two of the five were rented. I then called the owner and he seemed more anxious to sell. He said he had an Earnest Money offer for $44000, $5800 down, 10 % interest, which he wasn't accepting. I then invited him to lunch at Andy's

My Sixth Property - Daytona Apts.

Daytona Apts 1930

Dinner on 4th Ave. Before lunch was over we signed an Earnest Money for $44500, $5800 down, assumption of the mortgage balance $28560, $300 mo., 6 1/2 %, and a note for the difference at 7%.

The Daytona Apartments were sort of an exception to my purchase pattern. It did not show a return for several years but the financing was short term. I knew I had to feed it for awhile but the building was a "money maker" in the long term. The result was I subsidize the property with my return from my other buildings. It was helping me with my income taxes, and I felt I was working for the building for 13 years and then the building would work for me thereafter.

I immediately rented the 3 vacant apartments. There was absolutely no reason they were not rented before this as they were desirable apartments and priced right. I installed wall to wall carpeting myself in the studio because the floor was shabby. I installed a rubber backed material called Acrilan from Sears. It was a cut to fit carpet; no pad or tack strips were necessary. Shortly after that the material was not available anywhere. That was 1970 and the carpet is still there in the studio apartment today and looks great, 31 years later.

45

Next I went to work on the roofs. I put a new roof over the old garage roof using smooth roll material bonded to the old with lap cement. I then brushed aluminum fiber coating on top. The main building roof was 5 years old at that time, so I was told. I sectioned the roof and found it was tear-off, the old hot tar roof with gravel on top had been removed. A base sheet and 3 plies of glass material embedded in hot tar had been installed, with a flood coat of hot tar on the top. So I knew I now had a good roof except the only problem was the top tar coating was alligatored and cracked where the tar was too thick in places. I knew from my experience with the Northfield roof that it needed glazing. I got three bids and Walt Crow from Crow Roofing recommended aluminum coating, so I coated it with ACTO Aluminum Fiber Coating. I coated the roof every 6 or 7 years thereafter when the coating would flake and weather off. Also every year in the fall I went up on the roof and checked for cracks around the pipe flashings, hatch cover and parapet walls. I patched the breaks and cracks with mastic. Today I still maintain that roof and it's in good condition.

Next I tackled the central refrigeration system which consisted of a compressor in the basement with an evaporator cooler unit in each apartment. The cooler unit was an insulated metal cabinet about 2' wide by 3' tall and 2' deep next to the kitchen sink. This refrigeration system was inefficient, obsolete and was subsequently banned by the city. For example it would only keep ice cream frozen for about a day or so.

First I installed used refrigerators in each apartment. I found them in the want ads for like $40 to $75. It was time consuming to respond to the ads, go by and check the refrigerator out as best as I could, and haul them flat in my station wagon, but I was trying to save for another down payment on a building. I never had a problem hauling them flat in this manner because I always left the refrigerator upright for at least 45 minutes so the oil would run back down the lines into the compressor. I did buy a couple of refrigerators that didn't stay cold very long because they had been quick charged with freon but still had a small leak somewhere. I noticed the refrigerators that leaked out had a tap on the line near the compressor, a clamp on device,

My Sixth Property - Daytona Apts.

Income Expense Report From Owner - 1970

used for recharging. Thereafter I always looked for these taps and felt it was a high risk to purchase a refrigerator if it had been tapped.

The Central Refrigeration System was an ammonia system instead of a sulfur dioxide system. Both were commonly used in the 1910 to 1930 timeframe. The system was still active; ammonia was still in the lines, the evaporators, holding tank and the compressor. As an Engineer I had a lot of reference books so I looked up the characteristics of ammonia and found it had a strong affinity to water. Ammonia absorbs itself into water so I had a plan to tap into an

Thirty-Eight Years in Apartment Real Estate

```
                          ANALYSIS DATA
       BLDG     4504 Dayton Ave N
       ADDRESS   DAYTONA   APTS    1970
       Yearly Gross Income-----6900--         Projected----------

       Yearly fixed Expenses----------                  ----------
                                 65
              Elec.---------------------
                                 120
              Water, Sewer, Garb.-------                ----------
                                 842
              Heat--------------------                  ----------
                                 90
              Insurance--------------                   ----------
                                 711
              Taxes-------------------                  ----------
                                  —
              Other------------------                   ----------

       Estimated Expenses:
              Vacancy 2% of gross    138
              income----------------------
                                     276
              Repairs 4% of gross--------                ----------
              & Maintenance
                                    2122
       Gross yearly expense----------
                                 4778
       Net Income----------------                       ----------
                                 5100    1 @ 300 mo 6 3/4
       Financing, mortgage etc.-----    1 @ 100 mo 8%   ----------
                                 − 678   1 @ 25 mo
       Net yearly cash------------                      ----------

       Return %----------------------                   ----------

       Notes:
              • fast pay off may 13 yrs
```

Analysis Data

ammonia line and transfer the ammonia through tubing into a water filled laundry tub whereby it would just bubble itself off into the water and out the drain. As I started installing my tap into the line it suddenly broke the line and ammonia gas was spraying all around me and filling the basement with fumes. I quickly opened all the basement windows, doors and shut the furnace off because it posed a fire hazard. I then hooked up a garden hose to wash and transfer the ammonia to the floor drain. I started getting dizzy so I went upstairs to apartment #101 and called 911. The Fire Department arrived several minutes later and hooked up portable blowers to ventilate the basement and we cut the ammonia lines to the apartments so we could haul the refrigeration unit out into the alley. During cutting the

My Sixth Property - Daytona Apts.

ammonia lines, I was holding each line to steady it while a fireman cut the line with bolt cutters. Ammonia gas and refrigerant oil was spraying all over us and everything was a blur. Suddenly at one cut I noticed my first finger of my left hand was parallel with the line and protruded about 1-inch into the jaws of the bolt cutter. I got my finger out just in time as the scissor jaws closed.

As the firemen were packing up and leaving the supervisor said, "by the way which refrigeration company are you with?" I replied I was just trying to do it myself. Afterwards I thought I might get a bill for tying up a large fire truck and 4 fireman but I never did. My wife a nurse always said if I got in trouble or hurt working around my buildings to call the fire department.

The tenant that lived in apartment #102 was a retired Boeing Machinist who had lived there for many years. Both he and his elderly mother had originally rented the apartment and she had passed away several years before I bought the building. A year or so after I bought the building the retired machinist was shoveling snow off the sidewalk, which brought on a heart attack. He never recovered and passed away. Soon relatives started contacting me about getting inside the apartment to dispose of his things as the apartment was rented unfurnished. The relatives tore the apartment apart looking for the gold, or money, or anything of value. They left me a mess with a lot of Salvation Army type furniture to dispose of. They quit looking before his rent was up so I was able to renovate the apartment and get it rented right away.

A tenant on the second floor was a lady schoolteacher and soon allowed a guy to move-in with her. I've never had a problem with this even though it violates the rental agreement which read, 1 person in this case. I've always thought, and it has proven so, that if a good reliable tenant takes in a roommate- that roommate is probably a good person. So I just charge extra rent each month for the extra person. At that time the charge was $25.

Later my schoolteacher tenant called and said the refrigerator wasn't working. I checked the refrigerator out and could see someone had punctured a hole in the freezer compartment probably with an ice pick or knife to remove the ice build-up faster. A puncture leaves a smell of Freon and you see a yellowish oily film around the puncture, which is oil from the compressor. See maintenance chapter on refrigerators. My policy is I charge the tenant what the refrigerator is worth and they have the option to buy their own or I move another refrigerator into the apartment. In this case the tenant decided to buy their own and the roommate move it in himself. He was a big, powerful person and didn't use a dolly. He just picked up a 14 cubic foot double door Gibson refrigerator and took it up 2 flights of stairs to the kitchen. He even brought the old one downstairs and put it on the sidewalk where I flopped into my station wagon and hauled it to the dump.

In 1974 I leased a gas conversion burner from the Gas Company which saved me money over the cost of diesel oil and the associated maintenance. The Gas Company provided free maintenance with the lease program. Also gas burns cleaner so I didn't have to vacuum out the furnace flues and firebox very often. I used the remaining diesel oil in my tank by pumping it out and using it for parts cleaner and to cut (thin) my aluminum roof coating.

In 1985 my fuel cost was $4085 for the year. I hired the same electrical contractor, Burton Walls Electric, that converted the Northfield Block to electric heat to do the conversion. His company did an excellent job on the Northfield and had the best price. Like the Northfield the contractor installed a new service panel with new meter sockets, new circuit breaker panels in each apartment, extra outlets in the kitchen, living room and dining room, and electric baseboard heaters, thermostat controlled, in all the rooms. The total electric heat conversion cost was $8956. Again like the Northfield Block there was no change in rents and the electric heat conversion paid for itself in a little over 2 years.

When the Gas Company picked up their burner and I abandoned the hot water boiler I could not heat domestic water because that was provided by the heat exchanger on the boiler and piped to a hot water storage tank. I then leased a 85 gallom Rudd water heater from

My Sixth Property - Daytona Apts.

Daytona Apts 2002

the Gas Company to provide domestic hot water to the apartments. The Gas Company installed the tank and piping free. This new system cost me about $1200 the first year, which included the lease charge and the natural gas consumption plus free maintenance service.

In 1995 Seattle City Light had, and still does have, an energy conservation program whereby if you have electric heat, they install vinyl thermopane windows and pay part of the window and installation costs. In addition I paid the contractor $1375 to cover up or cap the old wood casings so there was no window painting left. It use to take me all summer every 6 or 7 years to prepare and paint the 60 double hung wood sash windows. The new thermopane windows reduced each tenants heating costs approximately 20% and greatly reduced my maintenance. The total costs including capping was $10646 of which City Light paid $3055.

December 1, 2001 I sold the Daytona Apartments to a apartment house owner who had bought 2 other properties from me in the past, Kirby Torrance III. I sold it direct for $520000, $50000 down, $3286 month, 71/2 % interest, all of which is of course public record.

Chapter 7

My Seventh Property - Dayton Apartments

In 1966 I was also after an apartment building near the Daytona, the Dayton apartments at 4420 Dayton Ave N. The building was built in 1909 consisting of 8 large 1-bedroom apartments, approximately 800 sq. ft. each with separate dining rooms. The building took up the entire 50 X 100-foot lot, including eves, except a 4-foot width across the back, (Setbacks were different in 1909). There were no sidewalks, no street paving, and just 1 set of wagon tracks in the center of the dirt road. A hitching post was out in front of the building to tie up the horses. I learned these facts from Mr. Lonsdale, the present owner who bought the apartment house in the 1930's and had pictures given to him by the former owner. Below shows a picture taken around 1930.

I liked the building. Mr. Lonsdale also owned 2 houses next door on the north side and lived in one since around 1925. Mr. Lonsdale seemed to like me and wanted to sell and carry the contract but I didn't have the required down payment at the time, so I bought the Francis Ave property instead. Lonsdale later sold his building in 1967 to a group called the TNT Investors (Tuesday Night Thinkers).

In 1972 I learned the Dayton Apts were again for sale by the owner of the Pauleeze Apts 59 units at 1st & Denny (now called the Arkonna). The owner of the Pauleeze and also the Dayton Apts was a schoolteacher, Richard Norman, who was in the apartment business for many years. It seems the TNT Investors assigned their equity in the Dayton Apartments as part of the down payment on the Pauleeze in 1969. The Dayton Apts were now for sale by Norman for $65000, $10000 down, $350 month, 7%. Norman and I had become

My Seventh Property - Dayton Apartments

Dayton Apts 1930

friends because his wife Bertie and my wife were in college together working on their RN degree and would meet almost daily to study together. I was able to buy the building direct from Norman (no Real Estate involved) for $53000, $9000 down, $350 month 7%.

The Dayton Apts fit my money maker criteria completely and more. It was and is today self-operating; tenant paid heat, hot water and electric. Below shows my analysis of the building at that time and it kept getting better over the 26 years I owned it.

The first thing I did upon taking possession was to send each of the 8 tenants a letter advising them that I was the new owner, where to send their rent checks, and a copy of my rental agreement for them to sign and return to me. All the tenants soon got together for a meeting to decide what to do about the new owner, so I was told later. The ringleader was an Electrical Engineer who wasn't employed, his wife worked instead and he stayed home and took care of the apartment. He wrote me a letter as spokesman for the group and included a list of repairs required in his apartment. In summary the letter said that they all had moved into their apartments on an "informal basis" and they refused to sign any rental agreements. I didn't respond.

Next I gave one tenant a 30-day notice to move because she had a dog (German Shepard) living with her and my policy was no dogs. She moved out at the end of 30 days taking an oak dining room table and 6 chairs that belonged to the apartment. I contacted the police who gave me a case number and said a detective would contact me soon. I never heard from the detective but she returned the table and 6 chairs a few days later. I was told that if I had not had an inventory list documenting the table and chairs that the theft would have been a cival matter. (See Chapter 10 How I bought the Park Apartments where the heirs moved out all my furniture and the police chose to do nothing about the theft).

Next I contacted the ringleader and made an appointment to inspect his apartment and proposed repairs. The first thing he said to me upon entering the apartment was that he had lived in New York City and had a lot of experience in dealing with landlords. I fixed what repairs I felt was necessary which was mainly a leak in the plumbing upstairs, the rest of his complaints were cosmetic. After that he was always around when I was working at the building, lounging on the front steps reading poetry, etc. One day when I was in the basement passing by his storage locker I noticed a pile of yellow rain gear, hat and a book titled "How to do Mountain Climbing". I learned a few days later that he had fallen 1000 feet through a snow bridge while trying to climb Mount Rainer.

All the waste lines in the building were lead plumbing. As I started getting leaks I knew what to do because of my prior experience with lead plumbing at the Northfield Block. The main leaks were in the 4-inch toilet elbow and 4 inch short line to the stack. Also cracks and breaks in the sink and bathtub lines where they joined the 4-inch line between the elbow and the stack. I started out by trying to wipe, scrape, and wire brush the lead at the crack area to get it clean and dry. Then I used coal tar mastic embedded in glass cloth to patch the crack. This worked and lasted for awhile but eventually started leaking again. I tried several other repair techniques including solder and wiping it to cover the break but I could never get it clean and dry enough. The glass cloth and mastic was the best temporary patch I found. Ultimately I replaced the lead toilet elbows and lines with ABS plastic with radiator hose sections and clamps at the plastic to

My Seventh Property - Dayton Apartments

```
                    ANALYSIS DATA
    BLDG     DAYTON APTS      1972
    ADDRESS    4420  DAYTON AVE N
                         $ 8174
    Yearly Gross Income----------          Projected----------
    Yearly fixed Expenses----------        ----------
                 hall lights   108
         Elec.---+ dryer----------
                             366
         Water, Sewer, Garb.------          ----------
                             - 0 -
         Heat-----------------                ----------
                             242
         Insurance-----------                 ----------
                             694
         Taxes--------------                  ----------
              8 leased water heaters (hot)
         Other + gas dryer        = 69       ----------
    Estimated Expenses:
         Vacancy 2% of gross      164
         income-----------------              ----------
                                 321
         Repairs 4% of gross--------          ----------
         & Maintenance
                                 1970
    Gross yearly expense-------              ----------
                                 6204
    Net Income----------------               ----------
                                 4200
    Financing, mortgage etc---               ----------
                                 2000
    Net yearly cash----------                ----------
    Return %-ON ON PMT $9000  = 22%          ----------
```

Analysis data - Dayton Apartments

lead connections.

The kitchens had old metal sink cabinets, drawers and large cast iron porcelain sinks with wall mounted faucets. Also several wall cabinets were metal and others were wood but all were too small. There was however a separate door on one side of the kitchens that led to a walk-in pantry. I remodeled all the kitchens using Pay-N-Pak oak cabinets and preformed countertops with stainless steel sinks. I installed shut-off valves and washerless faucets to reduce maintenance. This was a huge improvement over the old rusted metal cabinets and worn cast-iron sinks with wall mounted faucets.

The bathrooms had 7-foot long claw foot tubs. I found that ceiling and floor damage was cause by portable shower curtain hook-ups mounted in these tubs. I then went to a policy of not allowing these hook-ups because it was just to difficult and unreliable to contain the shower spray into the tub. Also these bathrooms were wallpapered and did not have exhaust fans so the excess moisture would lift the wallpaper. I allowed hand held hoses and nozzles for rinsing hair, etc which was always acceptable to the tenants and solved the bathroom damage problem.

In 1975 I had a fire in apartment #8 upstairs. The fire was a complete burnout with an 8-foot square hole in the living room ceiling through the roof. The fire burned through the ceiling and the Fire Department cut a smaller hole in the roof with a chain saw in the course of extinguishing the fire and ventilating the smoke from the attic. The tenant was a brakeman with Union Pacific Railroad and when he got off work he went on a "toot" along 1st Ave.

He came home later, turned on all his stereo, hi-fi, electric guitar equipment and later passed out in the bedroom. Luckily he had closed the bedroom door. When the windows blew out, flames were shooting through the roof, and the eves were puffing smoke all around, the neighbors called 911. The Fire Department arrived immediately, quickly put the fire out and saved the tenant by taking him off the second story bedroom window ledge. There was very little water damage to the apartment below, just a few water stains on the living room ceiling. The Fire Department used a high-pressure fog type spray to put the fire out. I got there about 20 minutes after the fire department arrived but I was just in the way as the Fire Department was hauling all the apartment furnishings out to the parking strip, so I left. Next morning my son John, 11 years old, and I went to the building expecting a mess. The Fire Department had cleaned out the apartment, wiped the smoke and grease off the appliances, and cleaned the halls and front steps. I felt so good about what the Fire Department did I wrote the Mayor and Fire Chief and received a nice response. The Arson Investigator said an overloaded extension cord to all the music equipment caused the fire. The cord had burned across the floor starting the carpet on fire. My insurance company handled the restoration in an excellent manner. They hired a contractor, Spurling Construction who specialized in this type of restoration. The insurance company negotiated several items such as: the last time the apartment was painted, age of the carpet, kitchen floor condition, etc. The result was I installed a new floor in the kitchen and pantry and the insurance company paid for the rest: new sheet rock walls and

My Seventh Property - Dayton Apartments

Dayton Apts roof today - 93 years old - well maintained

ceiling, new windows, carpeting, paint etc. Also I had loss of rents coverage. I felt the insurance company treated me more than fair. Actually the insurance was a joint policy split between Unigard and American Star.

The roof is today 2002 the original roof installed in 1909. (see photo of roof above). I know this because shortly after I purchased the building I sectioned the roof and found a heavy base sheet nailed to the wood decking and 3 plies of felt hot mopped with tar. The tar is pitch tar, like the tar that bubbles up from underground at the La Brea Tar Pits in Los Angeles. Pitch tar is different from asphalt tar, which is made from coal. Asphalt tar tends to crack with expansion whereas pitch tar is more soft, pliable and tends to seal itself in warm weather. The pitch tar plus a heavy coat of pea gravel is why the roof has lasted so long plus the fact that the roof has been well maintained. Another factor is there is a double wall foundation on the north and south sides with about a 4 foot passageway. This means a stronger, stiffer support system with less movement of the roof, a design technique used mostly in 4 story and larger buildings.

The parapet wall and cap roofing have been replaced many times. Leaks are hard to find in pea gravel but they are usually found around the skylights, pipes, chimneys and parapet walls. Sometimes a crack or

Thirty-Eight Years in Apartment Real Estate

Dayton Apts 2002

break can be 10 to 15 feet away and run along a rafter and drip onto the ceiling below. I have at times crawled around the attic to find exactly where the leak is coming from. Then I drive a long nail through the roof so I can spot it on top. A lot of times I've found the leaks on top where there is a blister or bubble. Then I would carefully remove the gravel looking for a break. If I cannot find a break at a suspected area I flood coat the area with 5 gallon pails of warm mastic or warm cold coating material. A Coleman camp stove works well for this heating. I prefer the mastic like ACTO Plastic Fiber-Seal #1714 better because it has fibers that tend to hold it together. Below is a picture of the roof today 2002, which is 93 years old.

In 1982 my oldest daughter was scheduled to be married at St. Brendans Catholic Church in Bothel one Saturday at 2PM. I had the flu, temperature of 102 and felt lousy. As I was leaving for the church I got a telephone call from apartment #6 that "water was pouring through the living room ceiling". I went to the church dressed in a brown tuxedo, gave my daughter away, finished the ceremony, and left the reception early. I changed clothes and went up on the roof to find the leak. It was cold, windy and raining hard. I was sweating from the fever. I couldn't find the leak source and I decided I probably couldn't fix the break anyway even if I found it because I had to

My Seventh Property - Dayton Apartments

wait until the rain stopped to get the break reasonably dry. I went into apartment #6 and stapled several towels onto the ceiling so I could control catching the water so it would go into 5-gallon pails. Next I went down to the basement to put the keys away and found 4-inches of water on the basement floor. A partial obstruction together with the heavy rain had caused the main sewer line to back up. I called Roto-Rooter who I always use and they came right out and cleared the line. This is the life of an apartment owner sometimes.

In 1991 I made my last payment on the Real Estate Contract and received a Warranty Fulfillment Deed, which I recorded at the courthouse. In 1998 after 26 years of ownership I sold the property myself to the buyer of the 4258-62 Fremont property, Kirby Torrance III. The price was $560000, $100000 down, $3537 month, 8-?% and he is doing well.

During escrow a problem developed whereby the title was not clear. I made payments to Norman and eventually paid the contract off and recorded a Fulfillment Deed at the courthouse. The problem was, Norman had a underlying contract with Lonsdale which when paid off was never recorded at the courthouse. The Fulfillment Deed was lost. Mr. Lonsdale had passed away. The Title Company said I needed a Quiet Title which would take approximately 9 months and cost approximately $1600. I then looked in the phone book and found a Mary Lonsdale , 94 years old, living in a retirement center, who remembered the contract with Norman was paid off in 1985. My escrow company sent Mrs. Lonsdale the required paperwork and she signed and returned it a few days later. Without Mrs. Lonsdale the Title would have been a problem because heirs were all over the country and hard to find. I must mention that in later years I always used John Wagner Escrow because they are great. John Wagner is an attorney himself but seems always available to help both parties, if necessary. All of his Escrow Officers I've found were excellent, but for the last several years I've asked for Prisca who I've become to know with quite a few transactions in my downsizing and she has been a great help. Any questions she has John Wagner as back-up.

Chapter 8

Money Makers

<u>What They Are:</u> I bought for maximum return because that plus the tax advantages of interest, expenses and depreciation write-offs gave me money back to re-invest and become financially independent. This just almost automatically pointed me in the direction of older buildings and fixing them. All the pictures in this book of my properties are "money Makers" because they are older style, reasonable rent, and close to bus and shopping.

<u>Older Buildings:</u> Older buildings, early 1900 to 1930, give tenants more space and storage for their money. They were built when materials and labor were cheap and the trades took pride in their work. During remodeling I've seen how the older carpenters did their arithmetic on the wood, sometimes barely readable but accurate. As a result, studs are plumb and parallel and square. The lumber was excellent in grade, without knots or defects. One-inch hexagon tiles were embedded in concrete on kitchen sink tops and bathroom floors. The Woodlawn Crest has hand painted wood doors, a technique used aboard sailing ships in the 1800's, a lost art today. Today the U.S. is a tear down and throw- away society. I visited England recently and saw first hand how many of their buildings were built in the early 1900's and some back into the 16th century. I think the majority were built in the 1800's - they don't tear them down - they maintain them properly and remodel them.

So older to me means built better with integrity, craftsmanship and quality construction. They can be found in any city I've been in across the country. It's easy to spot them if your visualize the pictures in this book. I believe quality construction stopped shortly after the

Korean War. The buildings built up to 1964 are the ones I would be after today, particularly the brick ones. After that the building emphasis was on maximizing the number of units on site and the cheapest, quickest construction possible. As a result, the siding leaks; wood rots and smells, the marblecrete cracks because of a bad batch, the roofs are flat to save money. Inexperienced architects use the rafter as the ceiling below and the roof on top whereas the quality buildings add up to another story to get proper water runoff. With flat roofs the standing water eventually penetrates the plies and leaks. One building next to the Daytona Apartments has had a new roof every 5-6 years because of poor design. My roof on the Daytona next door was installed in 1965 and I maintain it today 36 years later. These same designers believe that standing water would provide summer cooling and act like insulation in the winter - so I've been told. Now that we have torchdown material, it is safe with standing water on a flat roof because the material is very tough, yet pliable and does not become brittle and crack like asphalt. Torchdown materials are so new (20 years in Seattle) and they minimize maintenance so well we don't really know how long a torchdown roof will last if properly maintained. (see chapter under "Roofs" for more detail) I have torchdown roofs installed 18 years ago and they look the same today. They have been aluminum coated every 5-6 years for proper maintenance. I've never had a leak yet with torchdown roofing.

<u>Reasonable Rents:</u> Reasonable rent is what the average working person or couple is paying at the time. When I started in 1964 a one bedroom furnished apartment rented for $75 per month including heat. In those days it paid to furnish apartments to rent them easier. It seems there were more married couples then, going to school and working and wanted a 1 bedroom apartment furnished until they could buy a house. It was a trend until about 1980. You had to furnish the apartments and advertise and met them at the door and sell them. This of course gave me important feedback as to maybe why they weren't renting.

In 1980 things changed. There was more demand for unfurnished apartments. The average rent was $150 for either a 1 bedroom, furnished or unfurnished, with heat. Tenants wanted their own furniture even if they used apple boxes for bookcases or dressers for awhile with Salvation Army chairs and tables and couches. This was great for a landlord - we didn't have the cost of replacing furniture plus the expense of hiring help to move it in and out and dispose of it.

In 1983 another change occurred. Average rents with heat, unfurnished were $250. Furnishing hot water or steam heat was increasing in cost. At the Park Apartments my fuel bill was $6,144 for the year. I converted to electric baseboard heat in each apartment which cost approximately $16,000. Tenants didn't expect a rent reduction, the conversion paid for itself in approximately 2 1/2 years and the tenants were happier by better controlling their own heat. New wiring and extra circuits were included and the tenants liked paying for what electricity they used.

Today, 2002, reasonable rent is $650 for an older, well-kept 1 bedroom unfurnished, unheated apartment. There is more of a market now for studio apartments because fewer tenants are married, many work 2 jobs to make ends meet so they just want an older, well-maintained apartment for $550-575. They don't have much, just need a clean place to shower, sleep and get ready for work.

Since 1975 I've always had a steady supply of new tenants. Prior to then I had to meet them at the apartment and sell them. From 1975 and on, even when the economy turned a little sour, I always had tenants moving out of new, expensive apartments into my reasonable rent places.

<u>Close to Bus and Shopping:</u> I've found that tenants prefer a smaller apartment building (15 units or under) close to bus and shopping as opposed to large complexes. For example, when I bought the Woodlawn Crest in 1975 one-half of the tenants had lived there over 45 years. One lady, Edna Daw had lived in apartment #101 for 49 years. She was the Woman's column editor for the Post-Intelligencer Newspaper in the 1930's. I have one tenant who is still there today after more than 50 years in the same apartment.

So close to bus and shopping usually means long tenancies and if the landlord lives in the building, that's even better. (I personally would never consider it because you would never get away.)

Where They Are: We've established that money makers are "older buildings" with "reasonable rents", "close to bus and shopping" and "quality constructed". So if you look at my pictures you will see what and where they are. Everywhere I've been, city to city, I easily spot them. I used to go to Tournament Trapshoots and every city has them. In Lewiston, Idaho, for example, there are several that look like the Dayton Apartments, well-maintained and close to town. Every older city I've been in has them, built in the early 1900's. They are usually close to downtown because they are older and that's where the town started. A newer city like Bellevue Washington or Phoenix Arizona probably does not have many older buildings.

Why Buy Them: So now we've established what money makers are, where they are located and now we will discuss why buy them. First of all, people buy apartment buildings for many reasons. It boils down to love or money. Love means they like the things about the building, it's close to home, it first catches their eye, and so on. I've always bought for money reasons. So that's basically why I wrote this book - to describe how I did it. Whenever I've been caught up emotionally about a building I try to focus on the thought that first I'm in the "arithmetic business" not the apartment business. So if they don't add up I don't buy. I've given a little slack at times on my 15% return on the down-payment rule if I projected earning that in several years. I must say I've rejected a lot of great apartment houses because of my discipline. Those buildings would have worked out well due to inflation and subsequent appreciation, which translates into increased rents and profits. A lot of people buy for positive inflation and appreciation reasons. I've always believed in the bird-in-hand theory because it helps you in the business, you're there if inflation comes along. Money makers are great because obviously they keep pace with inflation. Also, when the economy turns sour for a while, I've always had a good supply of tenants moving out of more expensive apartments into my reasonable rent apartments.

Today, 2002, I would not buy an apartment house newer than 1964 because most are cheap construction, overcrowded and overpriced. The 1950 to 1964 apartments are the easiest to maintain in terms of plumbing, electrical, painting, etc. For example, you can easily paint a 1 bedroom, kitchen, living room, dining room and bath in one day (after the prep work) because there's very little brush/trim work. It's all flat work, few nooks or crannies, you just roll it out. A lot of the 1950 brick buildings still have a central heating system which is inefficient and obsolete and needs to be replaced with electric baseboard heat or in a few cases natural gas heaters if gas is already supplied for stoves.

The other reason is the new buildings since 1964 cannot compete with money makers because of the increased cost of materials, labor and financing. Today that translates into $800 to $1,000 apartments instead of the reasonable rent in the $600 range. Also, most of the newer buildings are smaller and overcrowded. I've had several tenants tell me they moved into a newer building and found their couch was too long for the wall space. The couch overhung the doorway and this was their reason for moving into a more spacious apartment.

Chapter 9

How I Found Money Makers

First I looked for an older neighborhood where well- kept houses were built in the early 1900's. Then I looked for apartment houses of the same age but among new construction. For example the Greenlake area, Woodland Park, Phinney Ridge looked good to me so I concentrated on looking for properties there. Apartment houses in close proximity to each other makes for a more efficient operation in my case, because I can never get all the tools or parts I need on the job so I have to keep going back to my storerooms. Now I am focused on an area how do I find apartment houses for sale? Well the obvious is through Real Estate but sooner or later Real Estate people realize its more profitable to own apartment houses than sell then. So Real Estate is always looking for the sleepers or good buys, either to purchase for themselves or maybe in partnership with a friend. The result is most properties advertised in the Seattle Times have already been scrutinized by investors, Real Estate people also, so the properties advertised are usually overpriced. But Real Estate cannot buy them all so I've found some good buys through Real Estate whereby the smaller properties have been overlooked by investors, usually because they don't want to work too hard for a good return.

I had the best results by driving around an area I liked and jotting down addresses. Then I would call one of the title companies for ownership information. I would then call the owner and see if they were interested in selling. If not, then I would call them frequently and build trust and develop a relationship. Several owners never sold to me but we were good friends for 30 years. But most are going to sell eventually and their prime interest is in selling to a responsible buyer they trust so they don't have to take the building back under

Thirty-Eight Years in Apartment Real Estate

foreclosure. I've bought many buildings this way, the Lilli Anne, the Park , the Woodlawn Crest, the Dayton Apartments, the Daytona Apartments and others. In my experience the best communication is between the buyer and the seller directly. There are exceptions however, sometimes it takes a third party, Real Estate, to put the deal together because some owners have no confidence and they want Real Estate to do it for them or go through their attorney. I believe I've had good results dealing direct because I've been there and I speak the owner's language. I negotiate, for example many times I've bought full price and made it up on terms. An example is How I bought the Woodlawn Crest where the owner had 3 earnst moneys ahead of me and I paid full price, but made it up on terms.

Another way I've found money makers and bought them is through the Sunday edition of the Seattle Times Commercial Real Estate section which it is now called. I've read this every Sunday since 1964 and still do. It's the little 2 line ads I look for which read "For Sale by Owner etc" because owners like me tend to undervalue there property when selling, but they appreciate talking direct to someone that's an "hands on" apartment owner. In every case I've found we have instant good communication leading to a sale that works for both of us. I've bought several apartment houses this way and I still look for the 2 line ads.

The advantage of buying direct from the owner who is usually retiring is buying on Contract or Deed of Trust, thereby no appraisal fees, no Real Estate fee, no points etc.

Chapter 10

The Park Apartments - How I Bought It

In 1969 one of the owners I contacted was Hartney Oakes who owned the Park Apartments at 4902 Phinney Ave N. The building consists of 12 1-bedroom corner apartments with separate dining rooms. Mr. Oakes said, "old boy doesn't require much care, long term tenants, low rents, no reason to sell unless I'm after something else."

In July of 1970 I sent Mr. Oakes a letter as shown below with my resume. I learned that he also owned the Malloy Apartments on 15th NE across from the University of Washington, 120 units. About 6 months later I stopped by the Malloy one morning and ask the receptionist/switchboard operator if I could see Mr. Oakes. He came out of the boiler room dressed in slacks, white shirt, tie and sport coat. I briefed him on who I was, how I'd like to be like him someday running my apartments full time. I was fascinated by my view of the boiler room as he had passed through the door and he offered to show inside. It was great seeing the hot water and steam heating plant. He seemed to like talking about the apartment house business, but he wasn't interested in selling the Park. I learned his mother had owned apartment houses on the south slope of Queen Anne for many years and he had grown up in the business with helping his mother and all.

I called Mr. Oakes a few months later and learned he went to lunch almost daily at Dick's Drive-in on 45th street. Except for Rotary and appointments he was at Dicks every weekday around noon. So I made it a point to stop by and briefly visit with him occasionally. He always bought 2 cheeseburgers 1 for his little poodle dog named Buttons and one for himself. For the next several years I managed to

> July 11, 1970
>
> Mr. Hartney Oakes
> 602 W Prospect
> Seattle, Washington
>
> Dear Mr. Oakes:
>
> As discussed with you on the telephone on Friday, June 4, 1970, I am interested in purchasing your building at 4902 Phinny Ave North. The exact price would depend on obtaining more information concerning the building, but I could pay $10,000. down and the balance on contract.
>
> The apartment appeals to me because its in a good location, close to the park, each apartment has a corner of the building, long term tenants and reasonable rents. I would like to care for the building like you have over the past years. My policy is to give immediate attention to necessary repairs. I always see the problems for myself, first hand, and if I have work done I always inspect the work upon completion. I wouldn't make any changes in tenancy or major improvements. I would plan to keep the building at least until its paid off.
>
> I would appreciate it if you would keep me in mind and if you have any questions please let me know. Attached is an outline concerning myself to give you some idea who would be looking after your building.
>
> Sincerely,
>
> R. C. Fenton
> 10417 76th Ave So.
> Seattle, Wash
> Sp2-2042
> work 655-4425

Letter to owner - Park apts

meet him at Dicks at least 2 or 3 times a month. Soon I was invited to sit in his El Camino and we had lunch together and talked about the apartment business. He had a lifetime of experience operating apartment houses and doing a lot of the maintenance and repairs himself. Soon I met Mrs. Oakes. Theirs was a good partnership; she took care of the books and rented the apartments, he took care of maintenance and repairs. At this time being elderly he hired mostly UW students to help him.

In October of 1973 during lunch Hartney mentioned he and the Mrs. were thinking of selling the Park Apartments. He said they would have to have $7000 a unit, which was a very good price then. We met and talked for 8 more months and I got to know his wife Ester. It was hard for him to let go of the Park as he had owned it since before World War 2, even lived there a short time while in the Seabee's, and had put a lot of himself in the building. I talked to Ester in May 1974

The Park Apartments - How I Bought It

```
Reginald C. Fenton
10417 76th Ave So
Seattle, Washington
Telephone: SP2-2042
Age: 38
Married: (18 years)
Children: Four ( 2 boys, 2 girls)
Employed by: The Boeing Co., 11 years, Engineer
             (wife is a RN at Providence Hospital)
Security Clearance: Top Secret
Present residence: 11 years
Organizations: Clarence F. Smith Lodge #482 F&AM
               Paine Field Gun Club
Present properties:                         year purchased
     House     10417 76th ave so            1959
     Duplex    2540 7th ave W               1964
     5 Units   4136 Woodland Park Ave N.    1963
     4 Units   4260 Fremont Ave N.          1968
     7 Units   4250-56 Fremont Ave N.       1968
     House     712 Mortor Pl N.             1968
Business References:
     Puget Sound Mutual, Second & Madison St, Seattle
          loan #8519
     Pacific National Bank, Wallingford Br.
     Prudential Mutual Savings Bank, Third & Spring
          loan # 7628
     Mrs. Gladys I Northfield 15821 75th Pl N. Edmonds
          RE Contract
```

Resume to owner - Park apts

and told her I felt maybe Hartney didn't have confidence in me to carry on like he would. She said "no that's not it I'll lit a fire under him," and she did. We closed the escrow June 1, 1974. The price was $79000, $16000 down, $500 month, 7%.

Housing and Fire Code Work

In November 1974 I received a "Notice of Violations" letter from the City of Seattle. This letter required many improvements to the Park building in terms of security, maintenance and fire protection. This action by the City occurred shortly after a fire killed 21 people at the Ozark Hotel on Westlake Ave downtown, the worst hotel fire ever in Seattle in terms of deaths, according to the press. The City then enacted Minimum Housing Code requirements in 1973 with all the laws for inspections, enforcement and penalties to upgrade substandard apartment buildings, 4 units or more.

I agreed completely with my violation letter. A major requirement was to provide one-hour fire-resistant doors to each apartment and 2 fully enclosed 1-hour fire-resistant stairwells between floors. The Park had 2 double doors in front and wide-open stairwells, about 8 feet across. I had 2 choices: (1) was to fully enclose each story with I-hour fire-resistant material; walls, apartment doors, fire doors etc. or (2) install a Fire Sprinkler System. I decided I wanted to keep the architecture of the building the same with the wide-open stairwells. This gives the tenants lots of open space while moving furniture in and out etc. Also there less space for intruders to hide as compared to story separation with fire doors. So I decided to have a Fire Sprinkler System installed which has the additional advantages of: gives the tenants a safer egress in case of fire, gives the Firemen a sprinkled access inside the building in case of fire, and increases the chances of saving the building by confining the fire to 1 apartment.

I got 3 bids for a Fire Sprinkler System. A company named Superior in Kent, Washington installed the sprinkler system in the halls, stairwells, furnace room and laundry room at a cost of $1969. It would have cost me almost as much to install new apartment doors, fire doors on the 1st and 2nd level, and story separation between floors. I was very satisfied with this sprinkler system and all I had to do was to paint all the piping silver for rust prevention and appearance purposes. Later the City required me to install an alarm bell, a water flow switch and pull stations at both front and rear entrance locations. Pull stations are special switches which when thrown activate the alarm bell. The pull switches cost $33.73, the alarm bell and electrical parts costs were $81.58 and I did the installation myself. Aside from meeting the City requirements, helping to save the building, the entire system may help save a life someday. I consider this Fire Sprinkler and Alarm System the best solution I ever made to an apartment house problem.

The rest of the violations were just routine improvements such as: new locks, peep holes on each apartment door, grills on the rear entrance door and windows for security reasons. The tenants of course liked the improvements and safety items. After all code work was completed I gave the tenants a $10 monthly rent increase and $10 the following year to help pay for the Housing Code work.

The Park Apartments - How I Bought It

Every apartment house needs a strong manager/tenant - Park apts 1977

I had the same type of heating system at the Park Apartments as I had at the Northfield Block. Central heat was supplied to hot water radiators in each apartment using a boiler heated with a Ray Burner employing PS 300 black oil. I leased a gas-fired burner from the Gas Company and eliminated the maintenance and saved money on my fuel bill. This heating system worked well but there was always a heat control problem. Tenants on the north side were always cold, tenants on the south side were always too warm. They all liked their windows open for fresh air. I was constantly adjusting the thermostat depending upon the weather.

In 1983 I hired the same contractor that did the Northfield Block to convert the Park Apartments to tenant paid electric baseboard heat.

Mr. Oakes had many years ago installed a new circuit breaker service panel with the capacity to convert to electric baseboard heat someday, if desired. At that time he converted all the kitchen stoves from gas to electric. This meant that the required wiring to each apartment was already there so new circuit breaker panels were added in each apartment and circuit breakers were added for the electric baseboard heaters. The total costs of the electric heat conversion were $15272.

Extra insulation in the attic was required by City Light, cost $2152. In 1982 my gas fuel bill was $6819. The improvement paid for itself in 2-1/2 years, a 44.6 % return the first year.

One time a tenant on the second floor called to say a rat had just came in the open living room window while he was watching TV. I said "Bill, you must get rid of the rat, we don't allow pets." So he did. Rats and also squirrels do have the ability to climb vertically up brick walls. The Park has a hollow tile type brick that has a rough outer surface making climbing easier for rodents. Rodents also climb smooth brick surfaces by hooking the mortar joints with their claws. Squirrels are better climbers. They can even climb downspouts so they can get to the eves where they chew the wood gutters to build a nest in the attic. One time at the Daytona Apartments I saw a squirrel climbing the 2-inch diameter downspout to reach the nest. I then greased the downspout and waited to see what would happen. Soon a squirrel came along, climbed the downspout, but about three-quarters of the way up to the second story gutter, he lost his grip and slid all the way down. He then ran to a telephone pole nearby, climbed up to the power line serving the building, and walked the line to where it was attached to the parapet, hopped down and then ran along the gutter to the nest. Squirrels are persistent and very destructive critters.

I had a water pressure problem at the Park Apartments due partially because the City water tank across the street at the Woodland Park Zoo is only 50-feet high and the pumps are not very efficient. Consequently, my pressure at the Park stays around 25 PSI. This low pressure is aggravated by long term rust build-up in the galvanized pipes in the building which reduce the volume of water flow. In 1994 I hired Quality Plumbing to install a new copper 2-inch water line from the meter to the water heater. Also 2-inch branch lines horizontally to the risers at the 4 corners of the building. Each riser of course serves 3 apartments in a 3-story building. This new water line proved very effective in improving the hot water volume to each apartment. The total cost was $2822 and I felt I had an excellent installation.

Also I found over the years that the main restriction in kitchen sink

The Park Apartments - How I Bought It

supply lines is where the 1/2-inch nipple to the wall-mounted faucet connects to the 3/4-inch tee in the riser line. I clean out the rust build-up inside the 1/2-inch nipple with a screwdriver. This greatly improves the volume of water to the faucet. If the faucet has a screen at the end of the nozzle this is the first thing I fix by discarding the screen. The screen assembly is a nuisance, always reducing volume because of catching rust and small particles in the city water system, so I throw them away.

Another time I had a problem of water volume to a toilet holding tank, just a trickle. I had earlier replaced the old ballcock/float with a Fluidmaster 400A, which are far superior. At first I suspected rust particles either partially blocking the shut- off at the floor or the Fluidmaster valve. I use a speedometer cable tool I have to enter and probe the line with the top of the Fluidmaster off; the shut-off valve open and the water shut off at the street. I detected an object in the line. Next I removed the supply line from the shut-off valve to the Fluidmaster. I found a pea size rock had worked its way into the City water system and was partially blocking the line.

In 1995 I signed up with the City Light Energy Conservation program to install vinyl thermopane windows with vinyl capping covering the wood casings. This was a threefold advantage at the Park: (1) energy savings, (2)-eliminated painting and caulking 84 windows and (3) reduced the street traffic noise. Phinny Ave is a very busy street with busses and cars going by all hours of the day or night. Now, with these new thermopane windows closed you hardly hear the street noise.

Another advantage is the tenants can remove a slider window, clean it, and reach outside to clean the rest of the window. The complete cost of the new windows installed was $15148 and City Light paid almost half, $7527.

One time I had a tenant that passed away and the heirs cleaned out the apartment taking all the furnishings that belonged to the building. When the tenant died I sent the heirs an inventory list of what belonged to the apartment. When I bought the Park most of the

Thirty-Eight Years in Apartment Real Estate

apartments were furnished. Mr. Oakes had bought a lot of quality items at Bushell's on 2nd Ave. Oak sideboards, oak and mahogany tables and chairs, leaded china cabinets, gold colored ornate mirrors were typical furnishings plus large older style dressers, lamps and nightstands.

Before the apartment was cleaned out I went inside and using a black marking pen I marked "PARK APTS" on the bottom of some of the larger items, such as the sideboard, china cabinet, dinning room table, etc.

A week or so later I entered the apartment and found it had been cleaned out. I called the Police and reported the theft. I had an inventory list signed by the deceased tenant and a copy of my letter to the heirs which I presented to the responding officer. He then called the heir and afterwards told me it's more a civil matter and there wasn't much the police could do. As a result I learned it's really up to the responding officer to choose to take corrective action and write a report and pass it along to the Detectives. At the time I was so busy completely renovating the apartment that I didn't pursue the matter.

Every 6-7 years I would prep, caulk and paint the old double- hung wooden windows and casings in the summer. My Boeing friends and others were going camping boating, fishing on weekends; I was painting windows. I never got done, all around, because of fall weather so I would finish next spring. I used a 40-foot ladder to access the 3rd floor windows. Years before I went to Rice Safety Equipment on 4th Ave So. and bought the safety equipment they recommended: a safety harness, a D ring ladder snap, and lines to tie the ladder to the roof and a additional mountain climbing rope with a clamp to limit my fall, about 2-feet if all else failed.

Also several months before the Park Apartments escrow closed we sold our house in Lakeridge and purchased a 5-acre mini-farm in Bothell, Washington. The 5-acres included a 3-bedroom brick rambler style home, with a 2-car garage, a two story old barn, chicken coups, and 2-creeks running through the property. It was a good place for kids, especially the 2-boys ages 8 and 13. We had a menagerie of farm type animals including; 1-goat, 2-horses, 1-cow,

The Park Apartments - How I Bought It

ducks, chickens, rabbits. Also 2-dogs, and 3-cats. A good place to raise kids in a country 4H environment. Oldest daughter Karon was away at the University of Idaho at the time.

Shown below is a picture of the Park Apartments taken in 1930 and another taken in 2002.

Park Apts 4902 Phinney Ave N 1930

Park Apts 4902 Phinney Ave N 2002

Chapter 11

I Quit My Job at 43, Now Its Full Time

In May of 1975 I quit my job to write my own paychecks. This was 11 years after I first started on the road to financial independence. I had a little more income from my apartments and stores than my day job. The purchase of the Park Apartments the year before really enabled me to be in the business full time and now I wanted to increase my income. I started by remodeling one of my stores. Sutton's Health Center shown on page 31 occupied 2-stores 1500 sq. ft. each with a doorway in back connecting the two. Sutton was using the north store for massage and storage for items he sold mail order and direct; such as gasoline additives to increase mileage, special rear view mirrors, massage oils, elixirs etc. The south store was his main office and business. He had a room partitioned off that he used for giving "Colonics." There was another area for "Vapo-baths," which employed a metal cabinet-like enclosure for a person's entire body to sit inside naked and inhale and absorb vapors. In the basement he had built a vaporizing system with piping (4-inch ducts) to each cabinet upstairs. There were 4 cabinets in a row on each side; on the right was a "men" sign and on the left was a "women" sign. A long, tall canvas curtain separated them. The vaporizer system consisted of a gas fired burner and holding tank above with a water supply and a tray to hold an Eucalyptus/Pine Oil mixture he purchased from one of the southern states. The system resembled an Octopus with 8 arms with a fire under the body. Sutton claimed great medicinal value from absorbing and inhaling these vapors.

I encouraged Sutton to consolidate his business into the south store at the same rent as the two stores, which was very reasonable then, $150 a month. I rented a 75-pound jackhammer and chipped out the concrete partial wall so I could install a door to the north store, 4254 Fremont. Then I installed a suspended ceiling with recessed lighting and then rented the store to an artist who lived and worked there for several years. Jay Kohn was his name and he did the 3-dimensional seascapes in his store, which were later installed at the Marine Aquarium on the waterfront.

Next I remodeled the kitchens at the Dayton Apartments using Pay-N-Pac oak cabinets and preformed countertops with stainless steel sinks. I installed shut off valves at the supply lines and washerless faucets to reduce maintenance. This kitchen remodeling was a huge improvement over the old rusted metal cabinets and cast iron sinks with wall mounted faucets.

Then I was able to buy another brick apartment house nearby, the Woodlawn Crest and I started work on the Housing and Fire Code Violations.

Chapter 12

How I Bought the Woodlawn Crest

In April 1975 I saw a little 2-line ad in the Seattle Times which read "Wallingford-10 unit by owner, $90000, $25000 down," etc. I called the owner and made an appointment to meet him at his building the next morning. He met me in the lobby wearing coveralls and quietly mentioned he had 3 offers on the building and pointed to his shoulder pocket where there were 3 Earnest Moneys hanging out. He then showed me through several apartments, the laundry room, and the furnace room. I told him I like the building, his price was fair, I wanted to buy it, and I have the down payment. I asked if we could get together tomorrow to sign an Earnest Money and put it in escrow. I told him I had rented a 75-pound jackhammer and had work to do that day. The following day we signed an Earnest Money for $90000 full price, $10000 down, $625 month, 7% interest. I was able to negociate a smaller down payment because if the impending Housing and Fire Code expense. The day before he had seen the jackhammer in the back of my old 63 Chevy station wagon, so after signing he said " a guy with a 75-pound jackhammer in the back of his wagon is the kind of guy I want to sell to." The deal closed 3-weeks later.

I took possession in May of 1975. As described previously in Chapter 8 half of the tenants had been there for over 45 years and all the apartments were rented. There was a central refrigeration system in the basement but it was an obsolete system. The coolers in each apartment would not keep ice cream cold for over a day or two. The first thing I did was to buy used refrigerators for each apartment just like the Daytona Apartments. The refrigeration system was a sulfur dioxide system, which is more dangerous to handle than an ammonia system so I hired a refrigeration company to pump out the sulfur dioxide into holding tanks, which they hauled away. I then hauled the refrigeration unit to the dump and removed the evaporator cooler unit in each apartment. The old refrigerator compartments in each apartment made good additional storage units.

One of the reasons the owner wanted to sell the Woodlawn Crest was he had received a Notice of Violations letter from the City requiring security and fire code work and he didn't want to do it himself. At this time almost every older building in the city had been inspected and received a Violations Letter which was also recorded against the title. I installed 5/8 Sheetrock behind each apartment door to comply with the 1-hour fire rating, new peepholes, and upgraded the locks. I had to enclose the first floor hallway and install fire doors at each end. The basement and second story already had metal fire doors at each end of the halls. The doors were sliders held open with fusable links. All I had to do was add smoke detectors and magnetic catches to hold the fire doors open. In case of fire or smoke the doors close automatically and the alarm goes off.

Joe Charesko an ex-prizefighter, lived in a studio apartment for over 50 years. He passed away there in 1976. The building was not security locked then and I noticed newspapers and magazines were piling up next to his door. I knocked repeatedly, rang his bell, but could not raise him. So I entered his apartment and almost missed seeing him as he had gotten out of bed with his shorts on and was lying under the Murphy bed on the tile floor. I felt he did this because he knew he was dying and didn't know how long it would take to find him, and he didn't want his remains to ruin the mattress and bedding. An empty bottle of Jack Daniels was on the floor near him. I knew he had expired and I could see rigormortis had set in because he looked stiff and was slightly bent face up. I called 911 and they first sent the Fire Department just in case he was still alive. Next 2 Detectives arrived and started going through his check book and personal papers. They found a savings account pass-book and a letter from a niece in California. Next the Coroner arrived with helpers who removed the body. The apartment was furnished but I had to properly dispose of the deceased personal property. I contacted the niece in California a few days later. The Police or the bank had already contacted her because she was the only heir.

The niece wanted me to give away or sell anything possible and send her the money, also any photos etc, which I did. In talking to her by phone I learned she was divorced, had just lost her job, had a small daughter, and sure appreciated the $25000. Uncle Charesko left her.

This was my first experience finding a tenant expired in one of my apartments. It's a shock to find them deceased but it's bound to happen and it prepared me for the next one. You have to be prepared to accept the responsibility and again the aftermath and procedures are well managed by the City officials.

One time I had a stopped-up bathtub drain line in a basement apartment. I tried all my tricks (see chapter on Plumbing) but could not clear the waste line. I went up on the roof and inserted my 25 foot long snake into the bathtub vent line, but it wasn't long enough to reach the obstruction. I then added a 15 foot extension to my snake using another snake joined to the 25 foot snake with about a 3 inch lap and 2 stainless steel hose clamps. This extension reached and cleared the obstruction but when I retrieved my snake the 25 foot section was missing. The coupling had become disconnected and the snake was still inside the vent line. I then used another 25 foot snake which wrapped itself around the missing snake and I was able to retrieve it. There was a big ball of hair at the end of the snake including one of the missing hose clamps. The other clamp is still in the line somewhere but has not been a problem.

The Woodlawn Crest has been a fun building to operate. It's like a magnet that attracts good tenants. Most of the time when I have a vacancy the new tenant is by refurral, someone in the building has a friend, or neighbors nearby like the building and apply. I've never had to advertise in the paper because a small "For Rent" sign in front gets good response.

Shown below is a picture of the Woodlawn Crest taken in 1934 and a picture taken today 2002.

How I Bought the Woodlawn Crest

Woodlawn Crest apts - 1603 N 46th St. - 1934

Woodlawn Crest apts - 1603 N 46th St. - 2002

Chapter 13

How Big Do I Want To Be?

In 1975 after buying the Park Apartments and the Woodlawn Crest I was even more financially independent, with 6 different apartment buildings, 40 reasonable rent apartments, and many long term tenants. I thought a lot about how big do I want to be? The last year at Boeing I was getting headaches, very severe at times. I was doing my best on the job but the overall responsibility was getting to be too much. I went to an Orthopedic Doctor my wife liked who gave me a complete physical and said "stress is causing the headaches, if you go to Hawaii for a week I guarantee you the headaches will stop." So I didn't go to Hawaii then but I quit my day job. I still had the headaches for awhile, but less severe, greatly improved, and the more deferred maintenance and repairs I did seemed to take the headaches away. That was 1975-1976 and I haven't had one since.

In 1974 during a yearly physical given by our family doctor he said my blood pressure was elevated at 130/90 and recommended more exercise. Specifically he proposed I start with the Canadian Air Force 5BX Program, a progressive series of calisthenics for physical conditioning leading to jogging. Soon I was jogging 1-mile a day, then 2-miles, then 3-miles a day for many years. This reduced my blood pressure to normal. I was particularly motivated to take better care of myself after seeing a retired Air Force Pilot die from a heart attack on my way to work at the Boeing Developmental Center. I learned he was only 43 years old. I was 42 then and have been jogging 6-days a week ever since. Today, 2002, I tell myself every morning the first and foremost important thing I do is run my 2-miles, everything else can wait.

So, while pondering "How big do I want to be?" I realized I needed

How Big Do I Want To Be?

minimum stress in my life and continued exercise. I didn't want to over-kill this financial independence thing and keel over with a heart attack at an early age. I wanted to be around to enjoy the rewards with my wife, 4-children and grandchildren.

In 1977 I was maintaining 57 apartments and things were going smoothly. We bought a summer waterfront home on Camano Island (see next chapter). I bought several other apartment properties and soon learned that about 70-units, 11 different buildings was about all I could handle myself, with my style of maintenance, like a 1-man band. I learned I wasn't very good at delegating responsibility. When I hired work done I just had to be there to make sure the work was done the way I wanted it. Consequently, with helper problems; not showing up on time, sloppy workmanship, etc I found the more helpers I had the harder I worked. I found my balance point, which is operating 50 to 60 apartments in 5 to 7 smaller buildings, like 5 to 13 units each because tenants like smaller buildings as opposed to large apartment complexes.

Chapter 14

Camano Island Waterfront Home - Tillicum Beach

In 1977 we started looking for vacation or weekend get-away property on Camano Island. We chose Camano because of no ferries and only 3/4-hours away from our home in Bothell. At first the most promising was a new A-frame cabin in the woods so we made a offer on it, but learned there was an easement that would have allowed a roadway 3-feet from our front porch, so we started looking elsewhere. Next we found a 1954 2-bedroom house on the waterfront at Tillicum Beach Drive for a little more money than the A-frame. We closed the deal at $57500 July 1st and started going there every weekend or so. Below is a photo taken several weeks after we bought the property, also a photo taken of the author writing this book, September 2001.

In the case of the Camano house, I learned that if you pay a little more for something you want, the extra price gets lost in the backwash. I've passed this advise along to my children and it proved to be a good example when later my daughter Karon bought 3- stores on Front Street in Issaquah at a slighter higher price than she wanted to pay. In a few years, with appreciation and inflation the extra money paid was insignificant.

Upon taking possession of the Camano house we found the place was alive with Carpenter Ants. They were nesting in a 2x12 beam above the fireplace. Using my wife's stethoscope I could listen to the ants chewing on the wood and sometimes they would poke their heads out of some of the holes in the beam. Carpenter Ants are about 1/2 inch long, solid black in color, and very destructive if nesting.

Camano Island Waterfront Home - Tillicum Beach

While they don't eat the wood, they build passages, tunnels and spaces for the queen and soldiers. They like to nest in damp moist wood like around a leaky toilet, shower or kitchen sink. In our case there was a long term leak in the roof cause by improper flashing at the chimney. Carpenter Ants are carnivorous and are always forging for food to bring back to the nest to share with the queen and others. Using Chlordane I sprayed a 3 foot wide band around the perimeter of the house which eventually killed some ants. The soldiers drag the dead bodies back to the nest, which when eaten, kill the queen. Once the queen is dead all the ants go elsewhere. I learned this from a data sheet obtained from the University of Washington.

Once every year I spray a band of Chlordane around the house. The first warm day in the spring usually brings the ants out. I see them inside the house and in the yard foraging for food, but they are only destructive if they are nesting. I've never had a nesting problem since I started spraying.

Prior to buying the beach house there were no vacations except 1-trip to Disneyland for the kids. From 1964 on, while my friends were boating, camping fishing etc, I was working nights and weekends, rubbing, scrubbing, painting, decorating etc, at my rental units. Each of my 4-children went often to the apartments to help Dad, mostly Saturdays and Sundays. The beach house was my token reward to my family for all the good family times they missed over the 13 years from 1964 to 1977. Also in appreciation to my wife for all the times we missed together while I was at the apartments. She loved the beach house, the waterfront, and the walks along the beach. We went there as a family unit until she passed away in April 1984 with pancreatic cancer. The rest of our family goes up there a lot, its like another world, yet only 1-hour and 15 minutes from Salmon Bay where I live. Weather permitting I can go by boat from my house on Salmon Bay to the beach house in less time than it takes to drive, and I avoid the traffic. Since then I met Jan Nielsen 3-years ago, a Ballard girl, widowed after 34 years of marriage, and she loves the beach house also. To follow is a recent picture of the beach house, my house and boat on Salmon Bay in Seattle and a recent picture of Jan and I in Alaska.

Thirty-Eight Years in Apartment Real Estate

Author's summer home - Camano Island 1977

Camano 2002 - a nice place to write

Author and new Mercedes at Camano - September 2001

Camano Island Waterfront Home - Tillicum Beach

Author's house on Salmon Bay - 2002

Jan and author - Alaska cruise 2001

Author's boat - Salmon Bay - on a lift - up to 12' tides here

Thirty-Eight Years in Apartment Real Estate

Chapter 15

How I Bought the Lilli Anne

In March of 1986 I received a call from the owner of an apartment building across the street from the Daytona Apartments, the Lilli Anne at 461 N. 45th St. The owner said he and his wife were interested in selling as they were going into a retirement home soon. I had contacted him about selling his building several years before but they were not interested in selling at that time. Also when I saw him at the Lilli Anne I made it a point to say hello and remind him I was still interested buying. Both he and his wife were retired missionaries.

The building consists of 4-2 bedroom apartments with a washer/dryer and dishwasher in each apartment, and a 1-bedroom daylight basement apartment. The building is all brick with aluminum windows, no yard work, off-street parking, low maintenance. Two of the 2-bedroom apartments have a fireplace and the other 2 apartments have 2-bathrooms each. The building was built in 1959; electric baseboard heat, separate water heaters, and the stoves are electric so the tenants get the lower all electric rate.

I purchased the property for $175000, $45000 down, Real Estate Contract for $81000, $1115 monthly, 11 %, and assumed an underlying contract for $49000, $433 monthly, 8 %. The $1115 monthly contract was a fast payoff- 8 years but it was what the owners wanted considering their age and going into a retirement home. This was an exception to my 15 % minimum return rule because I had a lot of surplus monthly income so I was buying on possible appreciation and I planned to pay it off early (see analysis sheet below). As it turned out I paid both contracts off in 1992 and today 2002 the Lilli Anne nets $34794 a year after taxes and all expenses. In addition the building

How I Bought the Lilli Anne

helped me with my Income Tax during those no return years. The Lilli Anne proved to be a good investment but I had to be flexible at the front end to meet the needs of the owner, otherwise they would not have sold. During the negotiation phase I learned that someone advised them to put the property under professional management which made sense, and I believe this would have happened if we had not reached agreement on terms.

Shown below is a picture of the Lilli Anne. Also an analysis data sheet when I purchased the property in 1986.

Lilli Anne apts - 461 N 45th - 2002

```
                    - 1986 -      ANALYSIS DATA
    BLDG      LILLI ANNE
    ADDRESS   461 N 45TH
    Yearly Gross Income------ $14555      Projected---------
                              3705
    Yearly fixed Expenses-----------                ---------
                               54
          Elec.---------------------                ---------
                              1423
          Water, Sewer, Garb.-------                ---------
                              - 0 -
          Heat---------------------                 ---------
          Insurance----------------                 ---------
                              2116
          Taxes--------------------                 ---------
                              1,2
          Other--------------------                 ---------
    Estimated Expenses:
          Vacancy 2% of gross
          income-------------- 291.5                ---------
          Repairs 4%of gross-----582                ---------
          & Maintenance
                                  4578
    Gross yearly expense-------------              ---------
                                   9977
    Net Income----------------------               ---------
                              18396
    Financing, mortgage etc---------               ---------
    Net yearly cash----------- - 8419              ---------
                              - 0 -
    Return %------------------------               ---------
```

Analysis sheet

Chapter 16

How I Bought the Juliana

In December of 1995 I accepted an Earnest Money on the 4258-62 Fremont property and was not really after another apartment building. I had sold the Fremont building to reduce my maintenance workload, and I had owned it for 28 years.

One Sunday after the escrow was in process I was looking at the Commercial Real Estate section of the Seattle Times as I always do, I don't think I have missed a Sunday edition in 37 years of seeing what is available, when an ad caught my eye. Near the end was a little two line ad which read "Ballard-13 unit brick, $650000, $250000 down, owner," etc. I called the phone number listed in the ad and an older male gentleman would only say "I know nothing about it, I just take messages." So I left my phone number. Several days went by and I had not received a call responding to my inquiry about the sale, so I called back again. At first I got the "he only accepts messages" routine but upon asking questions I learned approximately where the apartment house was, but as it turned out it was the wrong building. I kept calling the old gentleman every day or so and about 2-weeks after I saw the ad he gave me a telephone number in Bellevue. I called the number and a lady answered the phone. I told her about the ad I saw in the paper, that I was a serious buyer, been in the apartment business many years, I had the down payment saved, and would like the address so I could drive by the building. She said "my husband will meet you at 11 AM tomorrow morning, is that ok?" and gave me the address. Sometimes women are "really good at cutting to the chase." This process took about 3-weeks since I first saw the ad.

How I Bought the Juliana

The owner and I met the next morning. He showed me through several of the apartments. We were about the same age and we seemed to get along well. He also had been in the apartment house business many years. He and his wife had owned the Juliana for about 30 years. I told him I thought his price was fair that I would like to buy the property, lets work-up an Earnest Money and put it in escrow, so we did. I paid $250000 down, and assumed a mortgage for $400000, $2831 monthly, adjustable rate. As it turned out the timing was just right for a 1031 Exchange with the Fremont property thereby transferring my Income Tax gain into the Juliana.

The Juliana consists of 11 1-bedroom apartments, 2 2-bedroom apartments and a large garage on the south-east corner of the property. My actual return the first full year was 10 %, see below, but it only got better. In 1999 the return was 18.7 % of my down payment. The Juliana was built in 1964, all brick, and while it doesn't have quite the character as the Park Apartments or the Woodlawn Crest, it is an easy building to maintain. For example, a 1-bedroom apartment can be painted in one day, after prep work. This is because there is little brush work and every wall is flat without nooks and crannies and trim moldings; like the Park or Woodlawn Crest which take about 4 times as long as the Juliana. New vinyl thermopane windows were added in 1998, which greatly reduce the street noise. Another advantage of these windows is they don't steam up and drip condensation like the old aluminum single pane windows.

In 1997 I had a tenant that robbed a bank nearby. I learned from another tenant that one morning about 10 AM two Seattle Police Officers pulled up to apartment # 6 with a lady in the back seat. The officers brought the tenant out from apartment # 6 wearing a hat and had him try on several hats from his apartment. Suddenly the lady said, "that's him"! She was the bank teller that had just been robbed. The tenant had already given me notice that he was planning to move to Israel.

Next I received a telephone call a few days later from a person that just got out of jail. He said he met my tenant in jail and promised to clean out his apartment and that my tenant said he could have the

Thirty-Eight Years in Apartment Real Estate

TV and camping gear. I told him I would have to have this in writing from my tenant. He agreed and said my tenant was trying to contact but phone calls were very difficult to make from jail. He said he knew the system and he would go to the jail and get written permission to clean out the apartment. The next day he called and said he had the required paperwork signed by my tenant and notarized by an officer at the jail. I agreed to meet him at the apartment. When I got there 3 guys were waiting for me in a brown pick-up truck with Arizona plates. I felt a little apprehensive but the paperwork was valid and I let them inside the apartment with instruction to please lock the door upon leaving. As it turned out they not only cleaned out the personal property, they did considerable cleaning; stove, refrigerator, sinks, tub, swept the floors, etc. I sent him his full cleaning/damage deposit in a letter addressed to him at the King County Jail, 500 Fifth Ave. He finally was able to call me several days later and confirmed he received his deposit. He said that the bank robbery was a spur of the moment thing, that he had a flight scheduled to Israel the next day. He also mentioned the police were on him real fast because he used his own car and someone got the license number. He said he didn't even have time to count the money!

Sometimes I think I've seen or heard it all but something new always happens eventually.

To follow is a picture of the Juliana today and an actual data sheet showing the return the first year. 10.5% was less than expected but I had more vacancy than planned in order to straighten out some troublesome tenancies.

How I Bought the Juliana

Juliana Anne apts - 6308 24th Ave NW - 2002

```
                    ANALYSIS DATA  -ACTUAL -1997
    BLDG    JULIANA APTS
    ADDRESS  6308 - 24TH AVE NW
    Yearly Gross Income----73524--            Projected----------
    Yearly fixed Expenses----------           ----------
           Elec.---------------436
           Water, Sewer, Garb.--4488
           Heat-----------------0-
           Insurance-----------628
           Taxes--------------6778
           Other---advertising--202

    Estimated Expenses:
    ACTUAL
           Vacancy 2% of gross   1656
           income--------------1470
                                 4022
           Repairs 4% of gross-------
           & Maintenance
                                17604
    Gross yearly expense----------
                                55920
    Net Income--------------------
              INTEREST  29580
    Financing, mortgage etc--------
                          26340
    Net yearly cash----------------
                          10.5%
    Return %----------------------
                   ON $250,000 DN
```

Analysis sheet

Chapter 17

Maintenance, Repairs, Improvements
(there are undoubtedly more qualified people in the trades than I but, this book is simply "How I did it" and what my experience has been, and what I learned).

Roofs

In 1968 when I was at my day job if I had a roof leak I had several Roofing Companies I could call and they would find and fix the leak; Marchant the Roofer, American Roofing, and others. Along about 1974 it was hard to find a roofing company that would chase leaks, look for breaks and patch them; because of liability reasons and callbacks cost the roofing company money. For example, lets say a roofer finds the leak and fixes it, then another leak occurs near the first leak but the owner feels there should be no charge because its leaking in the ceiling below at the same spot as before. Roofing companies seemed to switch to a policy whereby they wanted to replace the whole roof. I understand their motive but the fact is the whole roof does not go bad all at once. Normally leaks start with small fractures or breaks along parapet walls, chimneys, vent pipes etc, because there is always minute movement due to thermal expansion and contraction. Next as the roof ages the oils in the felts dry out and become brittle, same with glass impregnated roll roofing, and the asphalt tar becomes brittle and cracks. Normally this occurs first on those areas that get the most sunlight because it's the ultraviolet light that ages the roof. So I gave up trying to find a roofer that would chase leaks. I decided I could save a lot of money doing it myself.

About this time, 1975, I talked to an apartment house owner, Roy Seger, about my roof problems. I had contacted Roy earlier about selling his 2 apartment buildings, the Ridgeview, 18 units at 50th &

Maintenance, Repairs, Improvements

Phinney, and the Sunset Heights, 12 units at 44th & Francis Ave and we had become friends. Roy told me he had been maintaining his own roofs since he bought his 2 buildings in the late 1930's. He used a glass cloth material, impregnated with asphalt, and aluminum fiber coating. Whether it's a patch or the entire roof you clean the area, lay down the glass cloth (comes in a roll up to 36-inches wide) and then brush on the aluminum fiber coating, applying several coatings with drying time in between. This produces a waterproof membrane that's good for 6 or 7 years and then needs another coat. An advantage of this aluminum coating is you can easily spot any breaks, just likes cracks in a road. So when you see a break or crack there is also sometimes a wet spot that is holding water and that is the leak source. Next I let the break dry out and then come back later and patch it using glass cloth and aluminum fiber coating.

The main advantage of the aluminum coating is that it reflects and blocks the ultraviolet light and lowers the temperature of the roof material all of which prolongs the life of the roof. As mentioned in Chapter 6 I maintained the Daytona roof in this manner for 31 years whereas the building on the East Side of the Daytona had a new roof installed every 6 or 7 years. I also maintained the Northfield roof, 5000 sq. ft. starting with the progressive bad places until I had almost 1/2 the roof over-coated with glass cloth and aluminum fiber coating. Also I covered the Woodlawn Crest roof with this same process which lasted for 20 years. Then the roof underneath, which never had aluminum coating, was so rotten that I had a contractor install a new torchdown roof.

When chasing leaks if you can catch the roof after a heavy rain when it's dried off you can usually spot the places that are holding water. Pushing on the area sometimes produces a squirt of water. It can be a pinhole size leak or a break. The roadway in front of the building is a good source to indicate if the roof is dry enough to spot the places holding water.

Sometimes, particularly in winter if I'm chasing a leak I take a gallon can of mastic and a small masons trowel and apply the mastic over the suspected spot. If I find a break that needs additional support I embed the mastic into a strip of glass cloth. ACTO Plastic Fiber Seal #1714 is my favorite mastic but Henry's is a good product also. I then come back in the summer/fall and aluminum coat all patches and look for additional trouble spots before winter sets in. In summer when it's hot and the roof is dry I don't use the mastic which is more for cool and damp conditions. For the aluminum/glass cloth process previously described the hotter the weather the better because the aluminum seems cook or absorb into the old roofing material the hotter it is.

In the early 1980's torchdown roofing material became available. Torchdown had been used in Europe for many years. The main advantage is it's a 2-ply system that eliminates messy tar. A base sheet is nailed over the existing roof and the torchdown material is bonded to the base sheet using a propane weed burner torch to supply the necessary heat to melt the underside and bond it to the base sheet. The seems are lapped about 3-inches and heated and bonded in the same manner. I had new roofs installed on 5 apartment houses in the mid 1980's. I let a new roof season for about 6 months then coat it with Karnac Aluminum coating every 6 or 7 years. I believe these roofs will last 40 years if properly maintained.

I've had good results re-roofing some of my garage roofs myself in the last few years using torchdown. I roll it out, nail it where the lap will be so the next roll covers the nail heads (3-inch lap), and seal, and bond the lap with a plumbing type propane torch. The torchdown is about 1/8-inch thick and so heavy it lays flat like a blanket. Torchdown does not bubble and crease like 90 pound roll roofing will do if its not bonded down completely with hot tar or cold application cement.

Plumbing
MAIN SEWER LINE BACK-UPS: tree roots cause most sewer line back-ups and the line needs cleaning out periodically with a 4-inch diameter cutter. However, I have a notice I posted at all my apartment houses which reads "Fragile sewer system- please do not put feminine hygiene products or dental floss down the toilet- they tend to snag and cause back-ups." I started posting this notice about 15

Maintenance, Repairs, Improvements

years ago and it's been a great help in reducing back-ups.

STOPPED UP SINKS: I learned the hard way many years age to put a bucket under the sink P-Trap before inserting my snake if the trap is not plastic. The metal traps can look good but are sometimes paper-thin and the snake goes right through. Then you have sink water all inside the sink cabinet, getting all the stored items wet, and water on the floor- a messy time consuming job to clean up.

First of all when I buy a new snake either power driven or hand operated, I throw the coiled ball end away. The coil is about 1/2-inch in diameter and it's of no use to me because it's too large to insert through the sink cross piece and secondly the ball does not snag the stoppage so you can pull it out. The ball just pushes the stoppage further out but frequently does not solve the problem and you have to get a longer snake. A 15-foot snake will clear most sink lines either kitchen or bath sinks, because they both drain into the stack nearby. Sometimes it takes a 25-foot snake to clear the line because the stack is further away or the horizontal line joins the main elsewhere. This is the case with the Juliana, the stack is 10-feet away from the kitchen sink but I cleared the stoppage approximately 20-feet out. When you buy a snake you can just unscrew the ball off the end of the snake. I then prefer an end that is just about a 1/4-inch radius bend or hook in the wire. This allows better control while running the line, not pushing but feeling the obstruction and I can also bend the snake for better insertion. For example, let's say I have a sink waste line that's back- to- back with the apartment next door. I insert the snake down the sink drain and it comes up into the sink next door. I then take the P-Trap off and put an additional bend in the snake end and feed it into the tee inside the wall and down the drain to the stoppage and then pull it back into the sink for disposal.

BATHTUBS: The old-fashioned claw foot tubs are usually not a problem to clear a stoppage. I first feed the snake into the tub drain then if that does not work I go down the overflow tube. If that does not work I look for a clean-out drum. Usually these are lead, about 5-inches in diameter on the floor near the toilet with a 4-inch diameter cover plate with a gasket and a 1-inch nut for removal. The stoppage in the drum is usually caused by a long-term accumulation of hair and debris. Getting the cover plate off can be a problem due to corrosion and age. I usually wind up using a chisel to take the pressure off the threads, then gently pry the cover plate off and replace it with a new plate and gasket. Then it's a simple matter to clean out the drum by hand. A snake will not do this because the snake enters the drum at the bottom and the exit of the drum is at the top so the snake just stops at the wall of the drum. Clean out drums can be hard to find. They can be inside a towel cabinet accessible by sometimes removing a floorboard. They can, in the case of Pembrook tubs, be under the tub accessible by cutting a hole on the Sheetrock or lath and plaster panel inside a closet. The newer Pembrook tubs don't have a drum. They employ a P-Trap instead, which can be very difficult to access with a snake because you run into a tee. I learned to use a combination of techniques. First I unscrew the stopper from the arm that opens and closed the stopper. Then I usually find a ball of hair 4 to 6-inches out. I go as far as I can with my snake. If the snake stops, and I cannot go further, and the snake comes back clean I then insert the snake in the overflow tube. If I go as far down the overflow tube as I can go and the snake still comes back clean I then give up using the snake. I then fill the tub with about 3-inches of water and use a large accordion style round plunger and work it up and down. If that does not work I hook-up a hose arrangement I made up to supply water from the bathtub spigot into the drain opening and stop around the hose with a towel using a screwdriver to make a seal where the hose enters the drain. Also I stop-up the overflow tube in the same manner and turn on both the hot and cold water. The water pressure, usually 60 to 70 PSI clears the obstruction. If that dosen't work I'd call a plumber, but I haven't had to yet.

TOILET REPAIRS AND IMPROVEMENTS: Toilets are a continual cause of maintenance and repair, A toilet problem can cause leakage and waste hundreds of gallons of water a month and if you have 5-10 or 50 toilets that's a lot of wasted water. What if you flush the toilet and the water is hot? I look for a mixer valve that's shot; usually it's the mixer valve in the dishwasher or the washing machine. Hot water is dominant so if the valve is bad the hot water is drawn into the cold supply line.

Maintenance, Repairs, Improvements

Ballcocks are a great design since Roman times, with the arm, float and shut-off valve, but when they get old the seat in the valve leaks and cause a furrow across the seat, which continues to leak even more. The float can leak and take on water so you have to bend the arm to get the required water height in the tank. I replace these with Fluidmaster 400A shut-off valves available in any plumbing department. Thereafter if you have a problem whereby the tank does not fill and shut-off properly its usually the rubber seat becomes hard and deformed with age. This rubber seat is a little larger in diameter than a quarter and is flat and about 1/8-inch thick with a protrusion in the center that accepts a needle like wire on the top side. Access to this rubber seat is by holding the main shaft with one hand and using the other hand to rotating the top of the valve 1/4 turn with the water shut off. It takes about 12 to 15 years of reliable service to where you have to replace this inexpensive ($1.50) rubber seat.

There is so much misalignment potential with the old ballcock, float, tank ball, guide and lift wires. I learned long age I reduce my maintenance if I also replace the tank ball, lift wires and wire guide with a flapper which is more reliable and has less chance to misalign and leak. In addition old toilets usually have corroded drain seats where the tank ball seats and seals. When the tank ball ages, starts leaking, the water causes a series of grooves or furrows across the seat. I learned the best thing is to take a flat fine file and draw it across the top of the drain valve where the flapper seats. This procedure produces a smooth flat surface for the flapper to provide a waterproof seal.

Now after I install a new Fluidmaster valve, new flapper, new stainless steel supply line, if I still have water dripping into the bowl I then know it's the rubber gasket between the tank drain and the bottom of the tank. This gasket also ages, becomes hard or disintegrates and looses its seal. Whether it's a 2-piece (wall hung tank) toilet or a 1-piece (coupled) toilet the problem is the same.

Toilet sweating is usually caused by the toilet running, leaking slightly, maybe not noticeable but cold water is continually going into the tank and bowl. The moisture laden warmer air in the room is drawn to the colder surface, which produces condensation on the bowl and tank, thereby dripping onto the floor. You can verify this leaking by putting a few drops of food coloring in the tank and see if it transfers to the bowl. The aforementioned repair procedures usually correct this problem unless there is some other influence such as lack of ventilation after a long hot shower, etc.

I always fix my toilets myself by using the tune-up procedures I've described at a cost of $6 to $8 dollars in parts. I buy the Fluidmaster valves by the case when they are on special at Home Depot or Lowes. They also sell flappers by the dozen at contractor price. The rest are 50-cent items like gaskets, bolts and nuts. Most people pay a plumber $200 to $300 for a new toilet, judging by the large number of used toilets I've bought for $7.50 at the Salvation Army on 4th Ave S. Another advantage to repairing an old toilet is older toilets have up to a 4-inch diameter throat and are less apt to clog up as compared with new toilets which only have a 2 1/2-inch throat.

RUST BUILD-UP INSIDE PIPES: Its typical in older buildings to have rust build-up inside galvanized pipes which supply hot and cold water to each apartment. This rust can build-up to where in a 1/2-inch diameter pipe for example, there is only a tiny hole for the water to pass through. The water pressure remains the same but the volume is greatly reduced. The only exception to this I've found is the Dayton Apartments built in 1909. These same type of 1/2-inch diameter galvanized pipes have little rust build-up. I believe this is because the water pressure at the Dayton is 85 PSI. The city would probably recommend a pressure reducer valve but the excess pressure has not been a problem. I believe the excess pressure has a cleaning effect, which reduces the formation of rust inside the pipes.

At some of my other buildings I had greatly reduced water flow at different locations inside the building. The water pressure at these buildings ranged from like 25 PSI at the Park Apartments to 65 PSI at the Woodlawn Crest. For example I would have good volume at the kitchen sink and the shower became a trickle, or the shower volume was good but the kitchen or bath sink was poor. I employed two

Maintenance, Repairs, Improvements

things to help increase the volume in addition to cleaning out the 1/2-inch diameter nipples that connect to the 3/4-inch tees in the riser lines as described in Chapter 10, Park Apartments: (1) I use a speedometer cable attached to an electric drill to remove the rust build-up inside the pipes where applicable, and (2) I use compressed air to dislodge the rust where the cable wouldn't reach. At first I bought a 125-PSI air compressor at Sears that worked well. I use a tire valve stem to connect from the compressor hose to the faucet or spigot. Sometimes taking the tub spigot off if necessary to reach the 1/2-inch diameter nipple. This compressed air blows into the open line, backs up the city water pressure and the cycling breaks up the rust. Sometimes it trips the relief valve on the water heater which is not a problem as long as there is a proper drain.

One time at the Woodlawn Crest I had a trickle of hot water in the bathroom sink in apartment B, and only a little volume at the shower head. Cleaning the shower head and using my speedometer cable at the faucet did not help. The partial obstruction seemed to be between the sink and the shower. I then cycled compressed air back and forth between the two with the faucets on and soon had an acceptable volume of hot water at the sink and shower. Rust particles poured out of the spigots and the shower nipple. I am presently working on a system whereby I introduce a small amount of fine sand together with the compressed air to help clean out the rust.

Most day to day plumbing problems are routine and there are probably many "How to" books out there but again this book is about "How I Did It" and the experiences I've had so I'm trying to avoid the obvious or routine. As mentioned elsewhere my favorite "How to" book is the Readers Digest Fix-it Yourself Manual. I've given a copy to several old timers in the apartment business, friends I got to know, and they too find the book a great source of ideas and troubleshooting information.
Another thing I've found is when replacing a faucet washer I use stainless steel machine screws because brass tends to crumble with age. Also I always burnish or dress the seat with a fine grinding cylinder about 1/2-inch in diameter with a 1/4-inch 3 or 4-inch long shaft to fit the opening and also fit my electric cordless drill. These grind-

ing cylinders are hard to find in that length but very handy and efficient. They're easy to find with a shorter shaft length so as I wore them out if I couldn't find the length I needed I just had someone weld on an extension. Separate shower valves require about a 6-inch extension sometimes. I used to replace the seat or take it out and draw the seat across a flat fine file until the groves are out, but later I found the grinding cylinder much faster.

Electrical
I learned early at the Francis Ave property that I could not always trust a circuit breaker. I had a burned out element in a water heater so I flipped the breaker to OFF and proceeded to disconnect the wires to the two terminals. I checked first to make sure the power was off by touching a screwdriver across the terminals. POW this blew the end of the screwdriver off. The circuit breaker contacts had fused themselves in the closed position. Also, since then I had times when I think I've shut the power off so I check with a neon tester, but if the power is still on its usually a case of turning off the wrong breaker.

I found a far easier way to change a water heater element than draining the tank. I place a towel on the floor under the element. I have the exact new element ready to install. I shut off the cold water valve going to the tank. I quickly remove the old element and install the new one. During the exchange the opening to the tank just gurgles once or twice with a splash of water because the vacuum is holding the water in the tank. Whether it's a screw-in or bolted type element this method is far easier and faster than draining the tank, and usually just wets the towel with a tea cup of water. If you forget to shut the water off you will find the water pressure is too great to install the element and by the time you find the shut-off valve and shut it off there is a lot of water to mop up. I've only had this happen once, unintentionally. I was in a darken water heater room using a trouble light and I forgot to shut the water off. While disconnecting the element a spray of water blew the light bulb out and I was in the dark scrambling to find the shut-off valve with the water rising on the floor. Once I shut off the water it was just reduced to a gurgle or two at the element opening in the tank.

Maintenance, Repairs, Improvements

I was an Electrician in the Navy, which has really helped me to do my own electrical work around my buildings. Large jobs like converting to electric baseboard heat, a new service panel, etc, I get bids and hire an Electrical Contractor. Routine jobs like light switches, new light fixtures, stove and water heater repairs, etc, can save a lot of money if I do it myself. A lot of useful information is in the Readers Digest book. I always turn the power off when practical but for example, if an older building has only one meter for 3 or 4 apartments, I sometimes don't shut the power off. I take the following precautions. I remember my Navy training which means; have your feet insulated and keep one hand insulated or in your pocket while probing around. What gets you is the electrical current across your heart or down your body, which freezes or paralysis you so you cannot release yourself and you become electrocuted or burned.

So it's hard to go wrong with the power off and something is not hooked up properly. Usually the worst that happens is the breaker trips. Sometimes breakers do not reset easily. I have to snap the toggle hard like flipping a light switch, really flip it hard. Then if no red shows and I don't have power I check the next upstream breaker. This breaker is usually at the meter service panel. Some direct shorts can trip the main breaker also, but usually the breaker in the apartment trips or the one at the meter.

Water Heaters

I found that most water heaters, gas or electric start leaking very slowly. The steel tank inside the cover and layers of insulation develops pinhole size leaks due to tank rusting from the inside. All my gas fired water heaters are either free standing in the kitchen usually next to the stove or they have been installed in the central furnace room. Where the gas water heater is exposed in the kitchen and a minute leak or wetting of the tank occurs inside the cover occurs, the tenant soon sees a small puddle on the floor. If a tank has had the gas shut off for awhile this puddle of water can come from condensation running down the tank and on to the floor, but with a hot tank the leak is cause either by a rusted out tank or a leak at the water connections at the top of the tank. These gas water heaters are usually removed and replaced without any water damage to the floor. I've never had one that leaked a large volume of water suddenly, always pinhole leaks that can go on for weeks.

Most electric hot water tanks however are located in a built-in compartment inside the apartment, either under the kitchen countertop or inside a cabinet elsewhere, sometimes in the bedroom at floor level. like under a linen cabinet. These can wet, seep, and leak for months then blow out a hole. The result is a lot or water damage particularly if the heater is on the 2nd or 3rd floor. When this large leak occurs carpeting gets wet, insulation in the ceiling below gets wet, as well as the lath and plaster or the drywall. The carpet needs to be taken up and dried usually using blowers. The pad needs to be replaced and the ceiling insulation needs to be removed and replaced. There are companies in the phone book that specialize in this type of restoration. I've always did it myself but usually hire help so I can complete the job faster with minimum disruption to the tenants.

Non-exposed electric water heaters are a problem waiting to happen. They say the average life of an electric hot water heater is 8 to 10 years but I've got some that are over 30 years old and not leaking. Still, eventually a slow leak or wetting will develop. I found I could buy a moisture detector, which is a smoke detector that is sent to Japan whereby, their converted into moisture detectors. The detector looks just like a battery-operated smoke detector but with a 4-foot cord with a probe on the end. I set the unit inside the cabinet with the probe on the floor next to the heater. If moisture occurs the detector goes beep, beep, beep, etc sounding an early warning. They are very sensitive to moisture. You can wet your thumb and finger, touch the probe end and the detector starts beeping. These moisture detectors are very reasonable in price. I bought some several years ago from Benla Plumbing. I remember the price was about twice the cost of a regular smoke detector and well worth the price. Batteries have to be changed every year or so just like a smoke detector.

<u>Refrigerators and Stoves</u>
Below is a notice I posted in the lobby of each of my apartment houses seven years ago regarding defrosting refrigerators. Since then

Maintenance, Repairs, Improvements

I haven't had a puncture. Until that time I used to get 2 or 3 a year. A puncture is easily spotted. I look for probe marks and yellowish stains in the freezer compartment which is refrigeration oil. Also there can still be an odor of Freon but my eyes are better than my nose. I've never found a reliable repair for a puncture in the freezer unit. Epoxy doesn't last due to dissimilar materials and thermal expansion so the refrigerant leaks out in 2 or 3 months. Aluminum gas welding could possibly hold but usually when a puncture occurs moisture is absorbed into the lines and blocks the flow of Freon. The best solution I've found is to dump the refrigerator because: gas welding, evacuating the lines, re-charging, sometimes a new compressor, costs more than the refrigerator is worth in most cases. Compressors are sealed units and are not repairable.

Dear Tenants:

HOW TO DEFROST A REFRIGERATOR. Remove frozen items and store elsewhere.

METHOD 1.
Turn refrigerator off overnight. Place pans and towels inside to catch water. The next morning it should be defrosted. Food will still be cold enough because the door has been closed overnight.

METHOD 2.
Place pans of hot water in freezer until defrosted.

CAUTION:
Never use a knife or any sharp object to remove ice. You can easily puncture the walls of the freezer as they are thin and made of aluminum. This will cause the gas (freon) to leak out and the refrigerator will not cool. REMEMBER IF YOU DAMAGE IT, YOU PAY FOR IT.

Sincerely,

B.G. Fenton

Since I posted this notice I've never had a puncture.

My policy is when a tenant punctures a refrigerator I first show them the evidence because sometimes they don't realize what happened. Then I give them the option of buying their own or I move another refrigerator into the apartment. Either way I charge them what the old refrigerator was worth plus $20 for removal and replacement which goes to my helper.

For the last 10 years I've been replacing refrigerators (when they're bad) with new 12 cubic foot frost free which eliminates the puncture problem. If a refrigerator is not frost free and requires periodic defrosting, tenants sometimes let frost build-up to where the door will not completely close. Also if it is a single door refrigerator with a separate freezer compartment door the frost can build up to where it breaks the door and/or closure mechanism. Prior to 10 years age I was always saving money for a down payment on another building, so I bought used refrigerators from private parties. I always plugged them in to check cooling and cycling. I learned to not buy refrigerators that had been tapped and recharged as they eventually leaked in a few months. Except for the tapped ones I never had a problem with a refrigerator from a private party. I always try to find out why they're selling it. Usually it's a case of the family has outgrown the refrigerator but it still has a lot of life left.

I always do my own repairs on refrigerators; thermostats, door gaskets, starter relays, fans, etc and save $60 to $80 or more on labor and trip charges. Its gotten to be a habit because I had to when I first started out.

Stoves
are very reliable and if there is a problem its usually obvious. I usually shut the power off because I'm dealing with 220 volts, very dangerous without one hand in your pocket. Stove top burners that don't work, I first look at the heating coils to see if there is any series of small protrusions or blowouts. If the coils look ok it's usually a broken or disconnected wire cause by the tenant cleaning the burner pan and disrupting the wiring. If it's not a wire problem I disconnect the wires and check the burner element for continuity with an ohmmeter. The same procedure applies to oven elements. Upon inspect-

ing the element if its not a blow-out or break in the tube and I have continuity I then take the back of the stove off and look for loose connections or broken wires. If everything is ok then it's usually a defective switch. I've only had one stove that checked out ok but kept tripping the breaker. That turned out to be a defective breaker, it worked at first but would not take a prolonged load probably due to faulty contacts inside the breaker.

Washers and Dryers

Some of my large 2-bedroom apartments have a washer and dryer in the apartment and I maintain them myself. Where I have a laundry room I've found it really pays to own your own machines even if you have to hire having them repaired. I've always purchased Maytag commercial machines or Speed Queen because they're both very reliable and don't change parts inside very often which makes them easier to work on and old parts can be re-used in newer machines. I have had times when tenants have complained of rust or stains on their whites and the problem always turned out to be a gearbox bearing seal problem. When this happens I either get a new machine or have factory authorized service fix the problem, which usually means a new transmission. My last problem like this was with a Speed Queen washer and the cost was about 1/3rd of a new machine.

Tuckpointing

The Park Apartments has a hollow tile type brick veneer. The brick measures about 5 1/2 x4 x12 inches long and has a 5/8-inch wall thickness. The original mortar is a soft mortar, which consists of 80% sand, 20% cement and a splash of lime. I use this same mixture because it seems to bond better to the old mortar than a hard mortar. Every year or two I go around the building looking for openings between the bricks where water is getting in the outer wall of the rectangular tile. I then spot tuckpoint these openings. I've found a Hi-Reach work platform is well worth renting at $200 a day to reach the 2nd and 3rd stories as compared to working off a ladder.

The south elevation of the Woodlawn Crest started giving me problems with the tuckpointing several years ago. Whoever tuckpointed the wall about 40 years ago didn't grind out the old mortar joint to a depth of 5/8-inches or more to get a good bond. The depth was more like 1/8 to 1/4-inch. Consequently, in winter when it rained water would leak inside the joint and when it froze the ice would pop the joint loose. I started getting water through the openings and running down the inside wall between the inner face of the bricks and the tarpaper covered wood . I then got 3 bids and hired a contractor, Pioneer Masonry to tuckpoint the wall properly. They did an excellent job. The cost of tuckpointing the south elevation from the cornice to 14 feet down including all sills and headers was $7134.

Flooring

I've always installed my own new kitchen and bathroom floor coverings. I sometimes hire a helper if it's a larger job like 9x11-feet with a lot of prep work. When I was in my 40's I did my own wall-to-wall carpeting installations myself but soon learned it's a younger persons job. Carpet layers and roofers really earn their money. I can do the shopping and be doing something else that's saving me more money then doing my own carpeting and roofing.

Usually I can lay a new kitchen or bathroom floor over the old. Sometimes this requires spot nailing and patching the bad spots and cracks with Fixall to get the floor as smooth as possible. Any bumps or irregularities tend to transfer through. I prefer shopping for good inlaid material, roll ends etc, although its harder to install, it last longer and does not tear like the thin vinyl material. When I buy the hi-gloss, no wax vinyl material I buy the best quality I can buy and this means thickness of the vinyl, not the backing. The vinyl material of course is easier to work with as far as forming and cutting is concerned as compared to inlaid which is 4 or 5 times thicker. I have learned its better to use a full spread material instead of the perimeter glue material because it lies flatter and is less apt to tear. I always sand the old floor first to get a better bond. Also I use lacquer thinner to remove any grease which is likely found around the stove area. I use a 40 to 50 pound roller, which helps to eliminate the bubbles. If I have a bubble I cannot smooth out I just stick it with a pin and then just roll the air out.

Maintenance, Repairs, Improvements

<u>Painting and Caulking</u>
I've been painting my own wood casings and double hung windows for over 30 years, until I went to vinyl thermopane windows with capping which covers all the wood casings. I painted my own because 90 % of the job is prep work; scraping, sanding, priming, caulking and I never found a painter willing to work that hard. Usually painters want to knock off the loose flaky paint and just overcoat the woodwork. Next year or so, after the painter is paid and long gone, the paint starts sliding off because the woodwork was not prepped properly. Since they took the lead out of paint nothing last as long so I went to the latex paints and primers because they are easier to work with and clean up is easier. A good oil base enamel with lead in the paint would last 10 to 12 years on the weather side, 30 years or more or more on the north and east sides. The best paints I've found are the Behr products. I particularly like the latex Deck and Fence stain for exterior woodwork because it weathers off with age and does not require scraping and sanding. For example, I painted the garages behind the Park Apartments with Behr stain 9 years ago and it looks the same today.

I always follow the trades to learn what they are currently using. In the case of caulking, when I got bids for the vinyl thermopane windows and capping I specified GE Silglaze II- 2800 Sealant which 7 years later is holding up well. This sealant has excellent 3-way stretch. The only problem it turns from white to black or gray depending on the amount of exhaust fumes. The Park has diesel busses going by all the time and the caulking is black whereas at the Woodlawn Crest there is less traffic and the caulking has turned light gray. I learned years ago that a small bottle of 50-50 solution of liquid detergent and water is very handy to have while caulking. I dip my finger in the solution and it helps tool the caulking into the cracks, aids adhesion and produces a smooth nice appearing joint without sticking to the finger.

For double hung windows where the putty is loose or missing I use caulking as described above because it is many times better and faster than the old linseed oil or plastic putty. After it's painted you cannot tell the difference. Silicone caulking has to season however before the paint will stick. Once it becomes less slick the paint will stick.

Vinyl Thermopane Windows
In 1995 I went with the City Light Energy Conservation Program whereby vinyl thermopane windows were installed. The first of 4 buildings converted was the Park Apartments. City Light normally requires the contractor to insulate under the first floor apartments, add a black plastic vapor barrier on the ground and install extra insulation in the attic but all this was accomplished, as required, when I converted to electric baseboard heat in 1983. Eighty-four new windows were added at the Park together with vinyl capping to cover the wood casings between the bricks and the new window frame. The advantages of these thermopane windows are: tenants save approximately 20 % on their electric bill, greatly reduced street noise when closed, eliminate painting and caulking every 6 or 7 years on the weather side, and all have screens to keep bugs, flies, rats etc out of the apartments. Also the slider windows can be removed so tenants can clean their windows on the outside if desired. The total cost of the new windows was $15054 installed, of which City Light paid $7527. The capping costs were $4987, which I paid. Aside from the aforementioned advantages or improvements the new windows give the building a nice appearance.

Now I had these new windows installed I found the apartments were sealed up tighter and subject to mold and mildew. I sent the tenants a letter as shown below titled Mold and Mildew. Since the letter to the tenants in all 4 buildings converted I've had far less mold/mildew problems.

Before I moved to my house on Salmon Bay in 1998 (see page 87), I lived on Sunset Hill for ten years. The first thing i did at the Sunset Hill house was to install vinyl theropane windows to enhance the view of the water and Olmpics. On page 112 is a photo of the house taken in 1928 and a photo of what it looks like today.

Wallpaper Repair and Texturing
Many older buildings like the Park Apartments built in 1918 and

Summary

MOLD & MILDEW

Dear Tenants:

    Now that we have thermopane windows installed, which seal up the apartment real tight, where does the excess moisture go? Well, its drawn into your refrigerator when you open the door so you may have to defrost more often. Next is mold and mildew may appear around your stove, refrigerator, bath ceiling, walls, around tub if your not careful. This is because if moisture has no place to go it will condense on these surfaces.

    HOW TO PREVENT MOLD & MILDEW. The excess moisture must have a way out of the building. When boiling water, cooking, showering, crack a window in the bath and one elsewhere so you get ventilation and let the moisture out. Fans are excellent. If you have plants they disperse 2 pints of moisture per day for a mediun size.

    HOW TO GET RID OF MOLD & MILDEW. Its a fungus which grows and loves warn moisture laden air. Cold air is dryerand prevents mold. ▓▓▓ or ▓▓▓ and soapy water plus clensers like ▓▓▓ on stubborn areas work well. Its the bleach that kills mold- ▓▓▓ and ▓▓▓ are just expensive bleaches.

    With a little attention to ventilating excess moisture you won't have a mold or mildew problem. The advantages of these windows in terms of energy savings, etc, far outweigh the mold problem which can be avoided with a little adjustment in life style.

Sincerely,

R C Fenton 6-20-97
R C Fenton   7-19-99

Thirty-Eight Years in Apartment Real Estate

Authors House 1928 - Sunset Hill

Author's House 1988 - 1998 added new thermopane windows

1909 respectively, have rough plaster walls and ceilings over lath. Instead of a finish coat of plaster, wallpaper was used. Therefore during redecoration new wallpaper was installed over the old. Then in the 60's and 70's it became popular to paint over the old wallpaper if it was drab, dirty or dingy. This was probably partially due to the fact that the old time paperhangers had passed on and labor became more expensive and painting is cheaper and much less messy and faster. Today it's difficult to find and hire a paperhanger.

When painting over old wallpaper I found if the number of different applications of wallpaper is 2 or 3 coats then the paint rejuvenates the glue. First I cut out the loose, cracked or torn places and patch them using drywall smooth tape and hot mud usually 40-minute type. I've found that hot mud is a lot stronger than the present drywall compound. After the first coat dries I trowel on a finish coat of light drywall compound which is easier to sand or use a wet sponge to obtain a smooth surface. I prefer a sponge because they are far less messy than sanding. I've found this procedure is far faster as compared to steaming old wallpaper off the wall, scraping the residual and either re-wallpapering or trying to finish coat the rough cracked walls and ceilings.

After I've prepped the old wallpaper as described above if there are uneven places I mix texturing into the paint and roll it on. Sometimes when wet you see bubbles but these stretch tight when dry. I always use flat paint on plastered walls because they are not as smooth as sheet rock and the flat paint tends to hide the defects whereas semi-gloss accentuates the defects. Also if the walls are really uneven I've had good results using drywall compound and a sponge and create my own swirl pattern, kind of a Spanish stucco effect. What was even better was asbestos fiber drywall compound because the fibers held the texturing together better and cracks were less apt to occur later. Due to the asbestos scare this material is no longer available.

Chapter 18

Policy - Smoking, Waterbeds and Pets

Smoking
I don't rent to people that smoke even if they say they only smoke outside. Some tenants can still detect a prior smoker and it's very offensive to them and some are allergic to it. The smoke permeates the walls, cabinets and carpeting. Even after the apartment is completely re-painted through out and the carpet is shampooed there can be a lingering odor of smoke. Until the ACLU gets a law passed or the Seattle City Council passes another discrimination law, I will continue to not rent to smokers.

Waterbeds
With waterbeds there is too much risk of leaks or floor damage. Over the years I've had several tenants sneak a waterbed into the apartment. When I find one I give them a "10 Day Notice to Comply or Vacate." Usually they put the waterbed in storage, but if not I start a court ordered eviction because there are those that live by the rules and those that do not.

Pets
For years I didn't allow pets in an apartment. I have never allowed a dog because it's unfair to the other tenants and dogs bark. If I allow one tenant to have a dog it's only fair to let them all have a dog. Size does not matter, they all bark and pretty soon if you allow one you have a building full of barking dogs and whats left outside is being tracked through the halls on tenants shoes.

I learned however that I refused tenancy to many real good people who had cats but this in my opinion was a mistake on my part. Many

Policy - Smoking, Waterbeds and Pets

people, particularly single ladies, look forward to coming home at the end of the day and being greeted by their cat and they really enjoy the cats company. Fifteen years age I changed my policy and I've never had a cat problem. The worst I've had is the cat claws the drapes or carpet but I just charge for this- no problem. Cats are very clean animals and a cat soon teaches the tenant to clean the cat box frequently. If not, what usually happens when the litter box is not clean the cat will go in the bathtub, in their owner's shoes, etc. I've just never had a problem by allowing cats and by not allowing a cat you eliminate a lot of really good tenants. I tell the tenant during the interview what I expect if they have a cat, aside from the cat box issue, if they have an outside cat they are not allowed to roam inside the building. The tenant must make their own arrangements to let their cat in and out of their apartment. Tenants sometimes get creative like several I've had built cat ladders from the ground to an open window and the cat quickly learned to climb the ladder. Just a 2x4 with 5-inch cross pieces every 6-inches works well.

One thing I learned is usually fleas, if any, go out of the apartment with the cat when the tenant moves out. There is a residual at times and it takes about 2 weeks to manifest itself. Fleas lay eggs, they hatch in about 2 weeks. We in Seattle have a law that we must return a cleaning/damage deposit to the former tenant with an accounting within 14 days of terminating the rental agreement. I learned that being conscientious and returning the deposit immediately after inspection was costing me money when 2 weeks after move out I had a flea problem found by the new tenant. It cost me $50 to have a flea extermination service spray and guarantee no fleas for 1 year. Willard Flea Service was the company I used and I'm sure there are other flea service companies that do a good job, but when Willard came out I never had a flea complaint thereafter. So now I withhold $50 from the refund until I'm satisfied there is no cat flea problem.

Chapter 19

Tenant Screening

I've never used any of the tenant screening services but it's certainly a smart thing to do and well worth the small costs involved. When I started I was not aware of this service to apartment owners so I worked out my own procedure which has worked for me, with a few exceptions. My procedure is as follows:

1. First I require an application to be filled out completely. I pay special attention to how long on the job and length of stay at their last apartment.

2. Then with application in hand I interview them starting with "are you prepared to pay your rent plus deposit in advance?" Any hesitation here is cause for alarm. Normally I allow a tenant to pay their cleaning/damage deposit amount as a deposit to hold the apartment for them subject to reference checking.

3. The selection of the proper tenant is very critical to the peace and harmony in my buildings, so I rarely make a decision until I have several applications, checked with their next to last landlord (the last one might say anything to get rid of them). Then if all thing's (criteria) are equal I honor who applied first and rent to them.

4. I have learned to go more by feeling or by my antenna (ESP) than what is on the application. I get them to talking about why they are moving, how they like the apartment, will there furniture fit, etc. Problem people seem to give themselves away the more you can get them to talk. Also, silence on my part after their answers usually causes or stimulates more talk such as; how hon-

est they are, how bad there last landlord was, etc. Sometimes I ask myself during the interview "why are they telling me all this?" and my thoughts usually are that they are good manipulators because they sound too good to be true.

5. In Seattle the rental laws strongly favor the tenant so when you get a bad one (loud music, belligerent with their neighbors, does not follow the house rules, no respect for others, etc) your stuck because of the Just Cause Eviction Laws. The City or the Police are absolutely no help. They say it's a civil matter yet the City Council crafted these laws that respect civil rights over property rights. So then I use ingenuity; give them their rent back if they move, plus full deposit, sometimes a bonus, etc. I cut my losses and get them out legally.

6. I sometimes consider their income to determine if they can afford the apartment but this is probably one reason I have not used a screening service, because with my low rent apartments the income amount has never been a problem. If a good tenant loses their job they soon have another, and if they are straight with me I carry them until they get solvent.

7. I am more concerned about behavior, consideration, respect, integrity, financial responsibility, honesty and my discussion with them during the interview helps disclose this. One fact in the landlord's favor is most people are good tenants. I've had tenants on welfare, Section 8 also, who were excellent tenants and proud they paid their rent on time or before due. In my 38 years I estimate the bad ones are about 3 or 4 out of a hundred, but beware of the 3 or 4. They can make life miserable and disrupt the lives of the other tenants in the building. I consider it critical to get the right one that fits in with the other tenants because I respect the other tenants. Some have lived there so long they have almost paid for the building.

8. I don't take applications unless they say they want to rent the apartment. Many times a prospect will say, "I'd like an application" so I say "does that mean your want the apartment and are

ready to put your deposit up"? If they say, "well I'm interested" I tell them I don't process applications unless they're ready to rent the apartment. Its surprising how many want an application but their undecided, like there shopping.

In summary, after I go through my aforementioned procedure I sometimes am undecided if I want to rent to a particular tenant. Something is bothering me and I'm not sure what it is. So I've learned when this happens I sleep on it, take other applications, and let mind work for me. It works every time if I let it work for me. Several times I've been wrong at first impression and after the interview, but after several days I was able to make the right decision. When you think about it, I'm giving the tenant an apartment for $600 plus $400 deposit on an apartment that's worth $100,000. The tenant has a lot of leverage considering the Landlord/Tenant Laws. In Seattle it's even worse because of the Just Cause Eviction Laws. The tenant can stop paying rent for up to about 3 months or more, depending on how quick the Eviction process happens, make life miserable for the other tenants, cook meth or deal drugs, trash the apartment. The City is absolutely no help; they just make the laws in favor of the tenant. The Police are absolutely no help; they pass all responsibility onto the owner. Then the best you can hope for is a Court Ordered Eviction enforced by the Sheriff, and a judgement good for 10 years against the tenant. Collecting on a judgement like this is a lesson in futility. An owner just has to be extra careful who they rent to and get the most information possible about the prospective tenant and be vigilant.

Chapter 20

Rents, Grace Period, 3-Day Pay or Move, Raises, Deposits

<u>Grace Period</u>
I learned many years ago there is only one thing that works with delinquent paying tenants- hit their pocket book! I allow a 5-day grace period, thereafter it's a $7.00 a day late fee. After the 5th day I leave a note under their door which reads, for example; "please leave your rent due on the 1st in my drop-box today or call me." If that dosen't get results and I know they are not out of town I post a 3-DAY PAY OR MOVE on their apartment door and mail a copy to the tenant. If they don't respond within 3-days I turn it over to Landlord/Tenant Services to start the eviction process.

Most, practically all tenants pay within this 5-day grace period. I think I've heard every excuse there is but occasionally I hear a new one. There are excuses and there are reasons. A typical excuse is "my bank messed up" or "it's lost in the mail" etc. A typical reason is "I just changed jobs and won't get my first paycheck for 2-weeks". Additionally, if they call me within this 5- day grace period, I feel their reason is valid and honest. I never charge a late fee if they are honest with me.

When I first started in the apartment business my first response when a tenant was 5 or 6 days late with their rent was to write them a letter or note which said words to the effect that I need my rents on time to pay my bills and the mortgage on time. Sometimes I would add, "shelter should be your first priority". After years of rent delinquencies I learned that this approach had absolutely no affect, that they would rather borrow from their landlord if they could get away with it. Then too I mistakenly thought a court ordered eviction would be expensive and time consuming so I listened to their excuses and tried to work things out with partial payments, etc. It wasn't until I started charging tenants, after a 5-day grace period, that I got good results.

<u>3-Day Pay or Move</u>
Twenty years ago I learned that there are companies that specialize in this eviction process and its inexpensive when dealing with a deadbeat tenant, or a tenancy that has gone sour, and you want them out. This is because the firms specialize in this process, with good clerks that do most of the paperwork on a high volume basis. Also one attorney may take 20-30 or more cases to court before a judge in one day. You can lose far more in loss of rents by listening to their excuses and promises to pay, than it costs in eviction proceedings. Also you eliminate the aggravation.

I serve the tenant with my notice, see as follows, which the attorney can work from if necessary. I serve the tenant my notice because it saves time, and fees and usually my notice, properly served, straightens things out because the tenant knows I mean business. After 3-days if rent hasn't been received I turn it over to L/T Services because I've worked with them before. Next I receive a Declaration Form to sign which says I properly served the tenant. Then the tenant is served with a Summons and Complaint. The procedure varies from here depending upon if the tenant answers or not, like contesting the eviction. Usually the tenant either moves or pays during the 1st or 2nd serving. If they pay after the 3-days you have to decide if you want to keep them or not because if you accept payment it voids the eviction. You risk starting all over again next month.

I've only had to start eviction proceedings past the 3-DAY PAY with four tenants in 37 years. Of these 4 only one went all the way whereby the Sheriff posts a notice on the tenants door stating that he will be back on a certain day and time to remove the tenant and their possessions from the premises. The owner is sent a letter that they are responsible to have a crew on standby to remove the possessions to the sidewalk. This I did but then the vultures came by so I made arrangements with Seattle Police Dept; a Community Services

Rents, Grace Period, 3-Day Pay or Move, Raises, Deposits

```
THREE DAY NOTICE TO PAY RENT OR VACATE  RCW 59.12.030 (3)


TO:




                                                    COUNTY: KING

     YOU AND EACH OF YOU are hereby notified that the rent for the
period below for the premises situated at the above address and county, is
now DUE AND PAYABLE in the following amount:

     Rent due on................for the period ending....................
     in the amount of:.........................................................
     Balance from prior months in the amount of....................
     Miscellaneous charges if any............................................
     Late charges if any..........................................................
     Charge for notice............................................................

          TOTAL DUE AND PAYABLE.......................

     AND YOU ARE HEREBY NOTIFIED and required to pay the above total in full
to the undersigned or his agent named below, within (3) days from the date
of service of this notice upon you, or in the alternative, to vacate and
surrender the premises.

     AND IN THE EVENT OF YOUR FAILURE to do so within the stated period, you
will be guilty of unlawful detainer and subject to eviction as provided by law.

THIS NOTICE ISSUED AND DATED IN SEATTLE, WA ON:

OWNER:                                    AGENT:


CC: LANDLORD / TENANT SERVICES
```

3-Day Pay or Move

Officer, to put the tenants possessions into storage nearby. This occurred in 1997 and the legal costs were as follows:

<u>Summons and Complaint</u>
$75 (server and fee's)

<u>Declaration & Unlawful Detainer Notice</u>
$50 (server and fee's)

<u>Writ of Restitution, Findings of Fact Judgement, and Order of Default.</u>
$258(fee's $150, Court $52, Sheriff $56.80)

If the tenant had moved after the 1st or 2nd serving the cost would have stopped at that point. So you can see the costs are minimal as compared to loss of rents for 2 or 3 months while listening to excuses.

Thirty-Eight Years in Apartment Real Estate

Raises

Since 1997 when utilities and property tax expenses started climbing, I started giving consistent, periodic raises. I think this was and is today the biggest management problem in the apartment house business. No one likes to give raises but if not given, expenses eat you up and devalue the building when you sell. Shown below is the form I send each tenant. Usually I've given raises each year and the increases were $20 to $30 a month. I've never had a complaint. Tenants know expenses and taxes are increasing and they expect a yearly increase just like their apartment friends. Also tenants expect a rent increase when a building changes ownership because of a new mortgage and I've never disappointed them. I always try to give them something first like new locks, deadbolts, peepholes, new mailboxes or some improvement.

I never had a tenant move because of a $20 to $30 increase. One time a tenant gave the raise as the reason they were moving but I learned they had already rented an apartment nearby, before they received my notice, so they were planning to move anyway.

With my reasonable rent apartments I always felt when a tenant gives notice there doing me a favor because I can paint or upgrade the apartment and increase the rent.

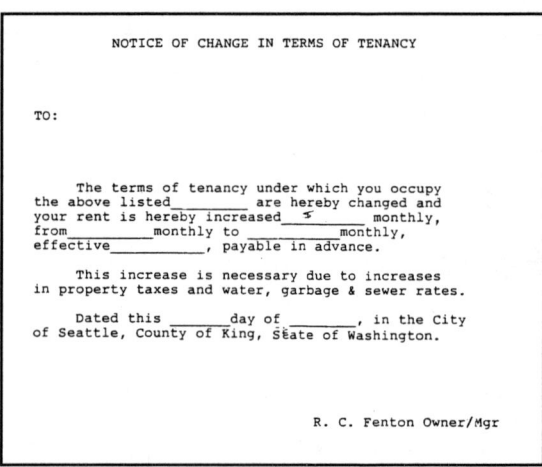

Raises

Rents, Grace Period, 3-Day Pay or Move, Raises, Deposits

One interesting fact is costs of utilities (water, garbage, sewer) as a percentage of gross income has remained rather stable, also property taxes. See chart below. This chart tells me my rents are keeping pace with inflation. The Park Apartments seems an exception with respect to property taxes but it's a large lot, 80' X 100' and has a higher comparable land value today.

Percentage of Gross Income
Utilities and Property Taxes

UTILITIES	1975	2001
Park Apts	10.2	9.9
Daytona	5.8	7.5
Woodlawn Cr.	5.3	5.6

PROP. TAXES	1975	2001
Park Apts	6.5	11.6
Daytona	11.2	12.8
Woodlawn Cr	7.9	9.9

Deposits

I've never charged the last months rent in advance. I've always felt that it costs a lot for a tenant to move; electric deposit, gas deposit, telephone, etc so I only charge the first months rent in advance. I never use leases because a lease only protects the tenant from a rent raise. If a tenant breaks a lease by moving I just re-rent the apartment because it's against the law to collect double rent anyway. I do however charge a sizeable cleaning and damage deposit. Today on a $600 apartment I charge a $350 to $400 deposit. Also with my older style, spacious units, unfurnished, by the time the tenants fill them up with furniture they tend to stay longer. Today I have several tenants that have lived in the same apartment 30 to 52 years. So this first month in advance, no lease, no last month, sizeable deposit works for me.

My deposits are completely refundable. When a tenant gives notice

```
        PROCEDURE FOR GETTING A COMPLETE
           CLEANING/DAMAGE DEPOSIT REFUND

DEAR:

        Your deposit _____ is completely refundable.
   Clean stove, refrigerator, floors, bath fixtures,
   mold around tub, sills, dirt, dust, lint. Leave
   keys plus mailbox key together with forwarding add-
   ress on kitchen counter.

        Let me know exactly when your out, I'll come
   by, inspect, and mail your deposit.


                                      Sincerely,


                                      RC Fenton
```

Refund procedure notice

minimum 20 days before their rent is due I give them my " Procedure for a Cleaning/Damage Refund", as shown below. Normally I find that a tenant is going to leave the apartment clean and a full refund is due. I normally have little cleaning to do, its usually a case of the tenant has been there so long the apartment needs painting, new kitchen floor, etc which is normal wear and tear.

A lot of times tenants are moving out/in on top of each other usually on a week-end so sometimes I have to do a little cleaning. Typically they forget to clean the oven, or underneath the stove, soap scum on the tub walls, or under the refrigerator. I do this myself because I don't know what I have until the tenant is completely out and then there often isn't time to schedule help. I then charge the prior tenant for this cleaning and give them an accounting and check in a few days (law requires within 14 days). Tenants sometimes overlook these intense cleaning jobs and hope the landlord will also. I always use a Check-in List and this gives a tenant a reminder of what to clean. For example if the Check-in List under Stove reads "Clean-burner pans, rims, trays under pans, under stove also" then if any item is not clean it's hard for the tenant to say "that's the way it was when I moved in". If I charge a $400 cleaning/damage deposit the apartment must be clean or otherwise noted on the Check-in List.

Rents, Grace Period, 3-Day Pay or Move, Raises, Deposits

```
                CHECK-IN LIST                    APARTMENT BUILD.

    CARPETS:

    WALLS:

    WINDOWS:

    CUPBOARD:

    DOORS:

    DRAPES:

    BATHROOM:

    APPLIANCE:

    OTHER:

    KEYS:


    TENANT ACKNOWLEDGES RECEIPT OF A COPY OF THE LANDLORD/TENANT LAWS.

    SIGNATURE...........................................Tenant

    SIGNATURE...........................................Owner/manager
```

Check-in list

Sometimes it works out that I pay the new tenant to do the cleaning and subtract the amount from the prior tenant's deposit. I've found the new tenants are so happy with the apartment that they are more than fair about the cleaning charge. In all the buildings I've purchased I've never seen a clean floor under the stove or refrigerator except where a new floor had just been installed. Usually it's a mess with grease, grime, food particles, cat hair, etc.

Chapter 21

Inspection Criteria - What I Look For

When I'm interested in buying a property and I've made an offer subject to inspection and approval, I do the following:

1. Request a rent role by apartment number.
2. Income and expenses last 3 years.
3. Check the foundation. If there is a crawl space I put my coveralls on and probe around and look for signs of infestation and dry rot.
4. Inspect the roof, paying close attention to; where the flat joins the parapet wall, around vent pipes, chimney, skylights, and the cap on the parapet wall which are all trouble spots. Also if the owner dosen't object I use a circular hole cutter to section the plies to see how many roofs are there and quality and condition. It's a simple matter to apply mastic and seal the hole.
5. Walk through each apartment making notes while checking: under sinks, around toilets looking for soft spots, tub walls for soundness and grouting, water pressure and volume.
6. Check the electrical panels, feel the fuses and/or circuit breakers to be sure they are not overloaded.
7. Then I walk around the building paying attention to the tuck-pointing, if any, also windowsills, caulking, headers etc.

After this I have a pretty good assessment of any deferred maintenance and problem areas and this becomes a work list to use in the final negotiation.

I prefer to do this inspection myself but there are companies that do this for a reasonable fee. I had a buyer one time that hired a firm to inspect the building and all the apartments. The inspector spent 2

Inspection Criteria - What I Look For

days, about 10 hours and found the minor problem areas in the building. When someone does these inspections every day they learn what to look for. I was told the cost of the inspection by a pro was $250 for a 10 unit, 3-story apartment house. The inspector offered to give me a copy of the report but after owning the building for 25 years he didn't discover anything I didn't know or considered important.

Thirty-Eight Years in Apartment Real Estate

Chapter 22

Shown opposite is a picture of my favorite Uncle Howard and wife Jean with the Pope in Rome in 1994. Uncle Howard was a professor at the University of California at Santa Barbara and became head of the Art Department until he retired. He lives in nearby Monticito which has some of the most beautiful and costly homes I've ever seen. Uncle Howard using the same principals as mine found money makers in Monticito. Restaurant workers, maids, butlers, gardeners, etc, need reasonable rent housing and there are some, but few. Most workers commute from nearby towns like Carpenteria or Ventura. My point is money makers can be found almost everywhere you have an older city or an older part of town.

Chapter 22

My favorite uncle Howard with the Pope - in Rome 1994

Thirty-Eight Years in Apartment Real Estate

Chapter 23

Drug Activity - Threat of Abatement

January 17, 2002 1530 hours I received a Certified Letter from the Seattle Police Department advising me of Drug Activity at one of my apartments and threatening me with abatement proceedings. First I called the Detective who was not available and left a message that I had no police powers, "what did the Police want me to do?" I never had anything like this happen in 38 years of apartment ownership. I called the Detective the next day but still no response after 2 calls. So since it was a Friday I felt it would probably be next week until the Detective got back to me and even if it was Monday I would

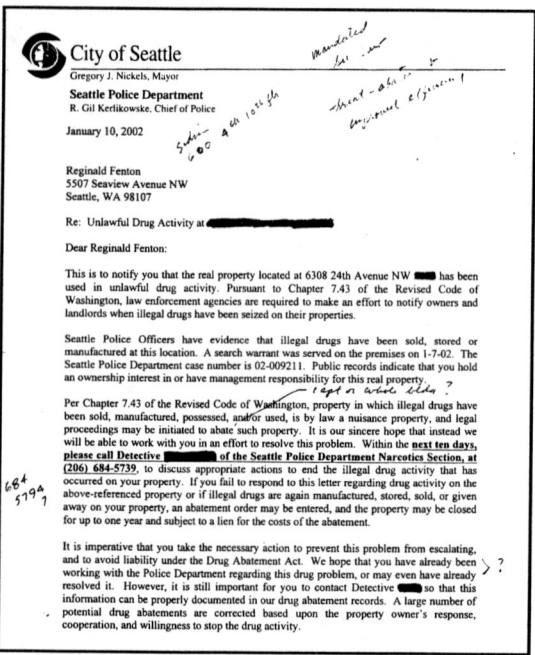

Drug activity - threat of abatement page 1

130

Drug Activity - Threat of Abatement

Drug activity - page 2

be one day past my deadline according to the Police letter. I then read the Landlord/Tenant Laws, both State and the unique Seattle Just Cause Eviction Laws and felt I was mandated by law to give the tenant a THREE DAY NOTICE TO VACATE see copy below. The names and address are obliterated for privacy reasons. I also request-

request for incident report denied

131

Thirty-Eight Years in Apartment Real Estate

EMERGENCY THREE DAY NOTICE TO VACATE THE PREMISES

TO:
▬▬▬▬▬
6308 24th Ave NW, Apt # ▬
Seattle, WA 98107

COUNTY: KING

SUBJECT: Unlawful Drug Activity at your apartment.

You violated the terms of your rental agreement which reads: NO ARTICLE OR SUBSTANCE shall be kept on the premises, nor occupation conducted which is illegal, noisy, or dangerous ....etc.

Today, 1-17-02 I received notice from the Seattle Police Department that a search warrant was served at your apartment on 1-7-02. The Police have evidence that illegal drugs have been sold, stored or manufactured at your apartment, case # 02-009211.

The Seattle City and Washington State Landlord/ Tenant Laws support this eviction. You have no other option as far as I am concerned. AND IN THE EVENT OF YOUR FAILURE to do so within the stated period, you and each of you will be guilty of unlawful detainer and subject to eviction as required by law.

THIS NOTICE ISSUED AND DATED IN SEATTLE, WA ON: 1-18-2002

OWNER: Reginald Fenton   *Reginald Fenton*

PS: Your deposit $325 is completely refundable subject to the Check-in List. Leave keys plus forwarding address on kitchen countertop. I will mail your Deposit plus balance of January rent.

CC: Landlord/Tenant Services
    Captain Jim Pryor, Narcotics Section
    Mark Sidran, City Attorney
    Captain Oliver, North Precinct
    Detective ▬▬▬▬, Narcotics

Corrective action taken

DISTRICT COURT FOR KING COUNTY
Seattle Division

STATE OF WASHINGTON)
                    : ss.   NO. _____
COUNTY OF KING   )   SEARCH WARRANT

TO ANY PEACE OFFICER IN THE STATE OF WASHINGTON:

Upon the sworn complaint made before me there is probable cause to believe that the crime(s) of VIOLATION OF THE UNIFORMED CONTROLLED SUBSTANCE ACT has been committed and that evidence of that crime; or contraband, the fruits of crime, or things otherwise criminally possessed; or weapons or other things by means of which a crime has been committed or reasonably appears about to be committed; or a person for whose arrest there is probable cause, who is unlawfully restrained is/are concealed in or on certain premises, vehicles or persons.

YOU ARE COMMANDED to:

1. Search, within 3 days of this date, the premises, vehicle or person described as follows: For the address of ▬▬▬▬▬▬▬▬▬▬, in the City of Seattle, County of King, State of Washington.

2. Seize, if located, the following property or person(s):

Any controlled substance as defined in RCW 69.50 to include, but not limited to marijuana and/or hashish; narcotics paraphernalia; items used to weigh, package, and prepare controlled substances for sale, distribution, and use; articles of personal property tending to establish the identity of person(s) in control of the premises; firearms used to protect and control the premises; where controlled substances may be found. U.S. currancy and other financial instrument that may be the proceeds from the sale of controlled substances.

3. Promptly return this warrant to me or the clerk of this court; the return must include an inventory of all property seized.

A copy of the warrant and a receipt for the property taken shall be given to the person from whom or from whose premises property is taken. If no person is found in possession, a copy and receipt shall be conspicuously posted at the place where the property is found.

Date/Time: 1/7/02 11:55   JUDGE _____

MARK C. CHOW
Printed or Typed Name of Judge

Search warrant

Drug Activity - Threat of Abatement

Inventory

ed a copy of the Incident Report so I would have back-up in case I had to go to court to obtain an Unlawful Detainer (see copy of Police Records Section response on page 131, whereby they refused to send me a copy).

The following Wednesday I was able to talk to the Detective involved who confirmed I took the proper action and sent me a copy of the Incident Report together with a copy of the Search Warrant and Inventory, see page 132 and above.

The tenant didn't contest the Eviction but requested to stay a few days longer for time to find a place and obtain help in moving. I agreed to this because I felt it was a reasonable and honest request so I didn't proceed with the Eviction process. The tenant moved and I learned that after being arrested and booked into Jail all charges against the tenant and roommate were dropped, yet the Police never told me, yet left me with a major problem. I feel like my drug activity was treated like a crack house in the central district, very heavy handed and threatening without proper timely notice to me. If the offense was serious enough to threaten me I cannot help but wonder why the charges were dropped?

After going through this scary process whereby the building could be closed up for a year and diposses all the rest of the good tenants, I absolutely don't see how I could have prevented this. The tenant had excellent references and had lived in my apartment for over 2 years. I think it was a case of a good tenancy that went sour. I later learned a roommate was taken in without my knowledge and that's when the marijuana use started I think.

Chapter 24

Then Vs. Now

I think of apartment houses as little gold mines. I've seen 2 apartment houses side-by-side, built by the same builder yet one is barely breaking even. The other is mining the gold. Like gold it's not usually where you can easily pick it up. It takes digging like good management, respect for tenants, proper screening, honesty in returning deposits, immediate attention to repairs and maintenance, etc, in essence a well maintained, well managed building. This requires a lot of work at times and as previously stated in Chapter 18 I was never good at delegating responsibility because I never found anyone who had my interest at heart, so I stayed small and did it myself.

I believe opportunities in Real Estate will always be available because a lot of owners are rather passive, they like the tax write off's, like to cash rent checks, but defer maintenance and repairs, etc, which erode the value of their properties. Even though my rents were comparatively low at the time I sold I always got top price for a well maintained building. An experienced buyer is only interested in his appraisal of what he can rent each unit for.

Long term owners tend to become complacent; fear a vacancy, don't give proper increases, put up with problem tenants, let tenants get behind in their rent, don't charge large enough cleaning/damage deposits, etc. When they sell privately their values are usually less than market value. Also it seems there are more 1st time buyers now than when I started. I think most of these 1st time buyers usually buy buildings they would like to live in instead of money makers. Consequently, sometimes the best investments like some of mine were overlooked. For example the Northfield Block was on the market for 2 years before I bought it. I think many just didn't want to do the work necessary to mine the gold.

On the road to financial independence I avoided several pitfalls. First, when I started doing well it was offers of partnerships. I avoided this because I've never seen a partnership that worked, except husband and wife and not many of those. Also I wanted to steer my own ship. One of my friends had a partner that faked his death and thereby caused my friend to go into bankruptcy because this situation ties up assets for 7 years. Another is a partnership that started before World War 2. One partner was a bookkeeper, the other in charge of maintenance and repairs. They had many apartments, about 1000 units I was told, but the partnership went sour. In this case the wives started the problem with statements like "my husband puts more time in the business than yours" and the partnership soon dissolved. Several other partnerships I've been aware of went the same way. Eventually one feels they're doing more work than the other is.

Another pitfall is they are successful in their business that they know and have worked at it for many years. Suddenly, they decide to open an entirely different business than the one they really know and they usually fail.

Another pitfall is the apartment house owner husband starts sleeping with one of the tenants; wife finds out, she divorces him, she now runs the apartment house, she gets the home and family car, he's sleeping in his Volkswagon (true story).

Chapter 25

Summary

The opportunities in Real Estate are the same today as when I started in 1964 because its an investment that gives you money back each year due to interest, expense and depreciation write-offs. Only the numbers are different but the percentage return can be the same today. Also, money making apartments are everywhere there is an older part of town and you buy right. How I found them, how I bought them most with owner financing has been discussed. How I made money making improvements and sold each one at a substantial profit has been presented. Appreciation help me a lot but mainly after the first eleven years after I became financially independent. After 1975 there were cycles of buildings doubling in value in 4 or 5 years. Of course rents kept pace with inflation and appreciation but this is the nature and pattern of staying in the apartment business for the long term. But for example if I can keep the Park Apartments rented today for $65 each plus inflation and property tax increases I still make a good return.

In 1975 when I quit my day job I was up at dawn ready to start my day. After years of getting up at 5:30 to 6:00 AM and going to work I always thought when I work for myself I would sleep-in a little longer. The new experience of being my own boss, coupled with the responsibility of maintaining my buildings full time, resulted in my bouncing out of bed at 5:00 to 6:00 AM eager to start my day. I felt needed; even if it was to change a kitchen light bulb for an elderly lady that had lived in her apartment for 45 years and was too frail to stand on a stool, I felt needed. How many retired people feel needed? I've always worked hard, fixing things, reaching and stretching, but it's a healthy lifestyle and keeps me feeling young. Working for myself has been the greatest reward in my life, next to raising four children.

Early on I learned it was far more efficient to set my priorities and concentrate on one problem at a time, like plan my work and work my plan. Also, I felt my mind was my best friend, always flashing solutions. I learned to attack problems in an aggressive, positive manner because solving a problem is the tool our higher power gives us to fashion us for better things. It's like we grow and become stronger and smarter with each problem we solve.

I hope the reader enjoys this book as much as I've enjoyed writing it. It's been my life for 38 years. It took me longer to get this book published than it took to write it. The major publishing houses seem to be only interested in established authors. I am glad I found Trafford in Victoria B. C. and recommend them for new authors.

ISBN 155395305-3